LET'S GET RIGHT TO IT!

Creating the lane in this digital game

Mindy Hill

Copyright © 2024 Mindy Hill
All rights reserved
ISBN: 9798344008332

Dedication

Please note that you always add value to any story because of your unique writing style, and how you convey the story to your audience. This is why I share news that you can absolutely use! Being great is achieved over a specific amount of time invested on enhancing your natural abilities. Here's to all my college years and the uncertainty of the media industry market shift to bloggers, but if you're not afraid to take a leap of faith during the transition, then you will grow into something as beautiful as a butterfly. – Mindy Hill, American Journalist

Acknowledgements

What is a journalist? It depends on who you ask. These days a journalist doesn't mean much too some people who have yet to be informed about what's going on around them. On the other hand, some people recognize a journalist as an individual who is trustworthy, has morals, values, knows the ethics of journalism, remains neutral and unbiased in their story telling, and has human compassion. Typically, there's some value in the story that has been published but most importantly it's authentic and true. And might I add, research is required even if you're not an investigative journalist. A member of the 4th establishment of government is also a journalist, and being recognized by the court of law is a great attribute to have especially in a digital world where ChatGPT can write a story for you then blast it as AI's own.

While attending the University of the District of Columbia, Mass Communications Journalism was my major. I had no idea that the market would shift drastically right before I graduated on May 5, 2010. The thoughts that would recur to me is what exactly was I going to do? It was too late to change professions now and those student loans weren't going to wait on me to figure out any next steps. So, what I did next was the best thing for me. And that was travel to Indonesia. My return to Washington, DC was with clarity and direction for my future in digital journalism. And I did just that! After spending roughly one month in Indonesia, upon my return I started *"Welcome to the Mindy Jo News Show,"* where I share news that people could absolutely use, so **Let's Get Right to it!** That was my signature slogan that I eventually trademarked. When I first started out, I didn't have theme music for my show. That would come later on when people saw that I was serious about my craft. Thanks to my friend Mr. Jay Smooth who lives in Atlanta for creating such an awesome song for me that's still the theme song.

Getting started is how you discover your gifts, talents, and special abilities that were granted to you at birth. So long to my college days of having a budget reviewed by the professor. And sending emails about extension of time for colleagues to turn in their stories for the online or print Free Voice news publication - where I served as Web Editor. My very first news show that I produced was uploaded to the communications networking platform YouTube. This is a networking platform allowed for account holders to have their own channel similar to like cable TV, that was a perfect fit for sharing information along with what I was doing, journalism- well so I thought.

The first show was inside my home on that July 31st day in 2013. I was sharing information about Facebook, lab grown meat, and mental health. While I was talking about mental health. The natural sounds of the ambulance in the background was great for the content. Starting out by yourself is not easy and asking for help can seem like a burden to some. I did have some assistance with filming periodically, but it wasn't a guarantee so I had to learn and apply all the aspects of the job. Yes, I did take video production classes in college, but the format was on VHS tapes. I would spend hours in the editing booth putting bars and tones on the tape then attempting to edit it, and still no picture showing. That's where I developed my skill of compassion for editors. Because the format had transitioned to digital requiring a very small SD-card to store footage on I had to learn editing software programs like Final Cut Pro and Adobe.

After publishing my first show, I learned quickly that outside was a better fit and feel for me. The second show was filmed on the porch. The vision of me leaving the porch and going in direct proximity to the people was very clear. I concluded that the people are going to make the show really pop if I ask good questions. Now as a journalist another rule is that you are only as good as your last question asked so to make it worthwhile. After the seventh show, my confidence was stronger, and I was comfortable with carrying this out from start to finish. I would later go on to produce over 50 digital news shows before my next big opportunity would arrive. During this time, I was able to host a symposium *"On the brink of Ferguson, the state of the Black Man in America,"* which featured Rev. Jesse Jackson as the guest speaker. I partnered with the Institute for African Man Development. This afforded me the opportunity to expand my digital portfolio and establish some credibility.

It was at the University of District of Columbia Community College Workforce Development program at Bernie Backus Campus near Ft. Totten metro station that the big opportunity would present itself. While sitting in the CompTIA A+ Networking Class, I was approached by Javan Steadham. He was also enrolled in the course. I then introduced myself and informed him that I'm a journalist producing my own news show. So I showed him my YouTube channel. He shared with me that he contributes to The DC Voice, an online news publication in Ward 5 DC. I thought it was incredible and we exchanged contact information. I didn't know much about The DC Voice. Obviously, I did find it was a beautiful seamless connection. And it was relevant to the university online news publication the Free Voice in the essence of capturing a "voice." I had a meeting with the editor of The DC Voice. Mr. Freeman and I met at a local restaurant in the Ward 5 community. While at the meeting I informed him of my pursuit of happiness and what work I had accomplished. Then I welcomed the opportunity to bring my talents to The DC Voice under one condition that *"Welcome to the Mindy Jo News Show,"* had to come with me.

After giving much thought and consideration to our meeting, Mr. Freeman sent me an email with the contract that specified the duties as a Web Content Provider in the capacity of a journalist. Some of the duties were to attend the Advisory Neighborhood Commission (ANC) meetings and get the website to the point where it's bringing in enough revenue to cover the monthly expenses and finalize advertising rates. This was a huge deal for me because work that had already been produced, and published, presenting the opportunity for endless possibilities, and it was paid. Although I was enrolled in the YouTube Advertising Partner Program, those pennies on a dollar didn't add up to a payout. And the program kept my $66.00 generated from Ad revenue in the clouds. I couldn't quite explain which content generated any Ad dollars because the

YouTube analytics wasn't accurate. Those are some dark clouds on that network.

But I was most excited about the freelance start. The job required me to work a minimum of 15 hours a week. No doubt I'd plan to do more hours because of my pursuit of happiness. These original beat stories are very sacred and special because they're what garner the statics of how I became one of the top producers of the publication. Not just that, the readership skyrocketed to almost 7% in my first year. That was tremendous because that was one of the goals we'd discussed during my onboarding as a freelance journalist for the online news publication. By the time I published my last article April 2019, the readership was very well over 10%. That's incredible considering Ward 5 is one of the largest populations in the District of Columbia. Oh, I can't forget to add, Google wanted to know how many articles I'd published and inquired as to why I received a pay increase. The editor informed their legal counsel that I was one of the top contributors, that's why! By the way, I had an alternative beauty regiment because I didn't have the time for a beauty salon every two weeks, so I often went with my signature look, a natural or braids. I did a little bit of makeup, but I'm so thankful the people accepted my true authentic self.

CONTENTS

Acknowledgements

Chapter One: CITY NEWS

"Edge City" Ward 5 Washingtonian's want More

Ward 8 Now Has a Sit-Down Restaurant: Busboys and Poets Welcomes the Community

Rooting DC Is Building Healthy Communities

'We Are a Community That Likes to Be Involved, Health and Safety Are Concerns

H Street Festival a Fantastic Community Celebration

The Cannabis Climate in the District

Donald Trump, Jr. Brings the Heat to Washington with the NRA

Mentors Making a Difference in the Metro City

P.A.I.N.T.S Covers the District

THE PANEL DISCUSSION

What's New, Affordable, and Healthy Living? The Wren

The Legacy of Marion Barry, Jr. Lives on in the district

Ward 5 Hidden Treasures

Chapter Two: POLITICS

Should the United States Foot the Bill to Rebuild Venezuela if the United Nations Failed to Act?

Mayor Bowser Promises a Fair Shot February

A Critical Conversation Continues Beyond the Symposium: Education in the District of Columbia

What Does Freedom Mean During the 157th Emancipation Day Celebration?

Sexual Harassment and Misconduct are Societal Issues or Issues Concerning Many Government Agencies Starting with USDA then the Forest

BLEXIT is making a Bold Statement by Breaking the Bondage of Political Orthodoxy in America

Turning Point USA Black Leadership Summit Revives the American Dream

Reform, rhymes and reasons for change in the criminal justice system

Reporting in the Era of Trump requires fair and balanced news

America's Most Unwanted Protest, Unite the Right

The Fight for White Civil Rights?

The DC Voice Talks with Ward 5 Candidate Kathy Henderson at the Wilson Building

Chai Tea and a Chat with Gayle Hall-Carley Candidate for Ward 5 Council

Justice for ASIFA Now

A Dream Deferred, Denied or Caught Between DACA and Dr. King

Will American Values survive a Biden Harris Election glitch Administration?

Chapter Three: TECHNOLOGY

America's Tech Giants Opt-Out of Idea of Being Regulated like Utilities

The Damage is Irreversible – Closed Captioning

Google's CEO doesn't know How His Company Operates – Needs Government Guidance

Getting to Understand Privacy from a Consumers Perspective 136

Who will Shape Consumer Privacy Laws Using Common Sense Standards?

TECH 2020 Helps Bridge the Divide Bringing Diversity to the Industry

The Damage is Irreversible – If it acts like a publisher...

US Department of Transportation Listens to the Public's Point of View on Automated Vehicles

The FCC Ends the Year with a Rollback Bonus: Ask your ISP for Details this Christmas

The MJ Experience: Enjoy Life and Learn, Tour Gallaudet University Museum

Did Artificial Intelligence Ruin the 2016 Presidential Race?

Positing Your Company to Sustain this Digital World

The Desk is Dusty in this Digital Media Era
Tools for Social Media

Fresh Start for the FCC

EVERFi and FISLL Ignite the Digital Era Launching FISLL 306

Caption This? Modernizing Wireless Phone Text Compatibility

Credibility in a Trend and Thread Society

The Content Controversy: Who Knows How to Ad?

IBM is Helping Move Government and Industry towards a Digital Transformation

Where Does the Value Lie: In the Institution, Student or Debt?

Keep It Simple, Central, and Smart, Access to Procurement

Online Merchants are mastering the Marketplace

Chapter FOUR: CULTURE

Cultural Heroes help keep art and culture alive in The District

Have you noticed how well trees treat us?

A sizzling summer fitness boost

A Refreshing and New Season: Springtime

Team Gary Russell Ready for Barclays Center

The First Friday of 2019

Urban Movie Channel premier subscription streaming service presents Jacqueline & Jilly

The Black Family Business – Ben's Turns 60

Major League Baseball's First base are the youth

Being ready is real when disaster strikes

Trill Grill Fest takes over D.C.

Russell still reigns as World Champion

Cypress Hill, Cannabis Clouds, and Cool Weather: It's time for a celebration

Black History Month continues because it's American history

Black History Month Film Festival

Celebrating Frederick Douglass during Black History Month

Is Black History Month still appreciated or declining in American value?

Hillary Clinton Honors White Women with a bash during Women's History Month

Bring America Back to Life

The DAMN Pop-up stops in DC

The DC Voice Attends MMTC 2017

The GAIL Movement connects with ISHTALK TV

Adopting a healthy lifestyle, nurturing the mind, body and soul

Fashion Trends in time for spring

ART Matters

Who's Right? Women and Transgender Women

Whole Foods Opens in Ward 5

Mindy's Movie Review

Chapter One

CITY NEWS

To get the full reader's interactive experience, you will need a few materials:

1) An open mind

2) Smart Phone – any brand that affords you access to the internet; or

3) Tablet – must have access to the internet; or

4) Desktop computer – must have access to the internet; or

5) Laptop – must have access to the internet

When you see a video camera on the page, please use your electronic device to enter either

YouTube.com or Vimeo.com website. Then in the search bar type in the title provided to watch the digital news content which has been created and curated for that article. If a video camera is not shown on the page, simply envision what the scene would look like, or you can get creative and draw your own scene. No matter the brevity or depth, breaking boundaries in the digital media news era creating the wave has been most inspiring, important, impactful and igniting for developing a lane to sustain such exceptional bodies of work, giving the reader a different view and interactive experience.

MJ News Update: Because this would be my first article published on The DC Voice website I wanted to connect to the community. Looking back at the article it was pretty good for the first one and relevant to the jurisdiction in which my core readers existed. Ward 5 in the District of Columbia has the largest population in the city, so it was a great way to introduce myself also.

"Edge City" Ward 5 Washingtonian's Want More

The culture and heritage of Ward 5 resounds around the district in the midst of the constant change and city plan phases. What's often unanswered are the wants and needs of the residents of the largest ward in the District of Columbia, Ward 5. Whether it's riding metro, going to work, attending events at the Mayflower Renaissance Hotel, or maintaining a company's computer, Ward 5 Washingtonian's are moving and making things happen in the District of Columbia, but whose addressing their community needs, wants, and desires? While at the Mayflower Hotel Marcus Hughes, a DC transplant now a Ward 5 resident was asked *"What do you want to see happen for Ward 5?"* He replied, *"I am starting to see more gentrification near Brentwood Manor and as Ward 5 advances people will not be able to keep up with the financial changes around them."* Mr. Hughes attends the University of the District of Columbia with a curriculum focus on Political Science and Pre-Law. Luckily, for Mr. Hughes he knows to call on his Council member Kenyan McDuffie if in need of constituent services since he did contact their office for energy assistance, and Council member McDuffie's office was able to provide the necessary assistance.

Ward 5 is constantly changing with new business and more developments. Sometimes change is good, but change can create some not so cost-effective circumstances, and this seems to be a concern of Ward 5 resident Jackie Dye. Ms. Dye who was raised in Ward 5 and works for a hotel wants to see lower housing she says, *"make it affordable."* She along with a group of concerned workers plan to meet with Council member-at –large Vincent Orange to address their concerns of the new online hotel company Airbnb's contract "we don't think it's fair taking away jobs," says Ms. Dye.

Born at Washington Hospital Center, Ward 5 Washingtonian Timothy Barnes wants the days of affordable housing to resonate when he attended elementary school at Emory. Mr. Barnes says "I don't like how the cost of living is raising the price of homes has doubled from $350,000 to $600,000 then sell the home for $1.4 million dollars." Maybe McDuffie can figure out a plan to help combat the issue of affordable housing. Mr. Barnes has contacted the Council member's office for constituent services and Council member McDuffie's office was prompt with responding and addressing his needs.

Residents of Ward 5 like the convenience and access to metro, however Saidu Kamara wants to see a change in the area like the abandon buildings that they could turn into something else. Mr. Kamara isn't quite familiar with his Council member's office and says he would forget to contact their office. What also seems to be forgotten are some of the wants and needs of Washingtonian's in "Edge City."

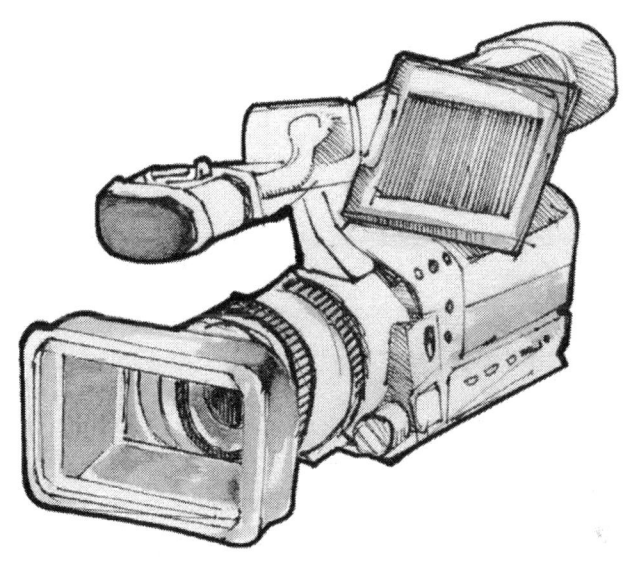

Title: Busboys and Poets Is Open in Ward 8

Interactive Source: YouTube.com

Original Production Year: **2019**

<u>MJ News Update:</u> This was a surprise to me that Ward 8 had been unable to experience having the luxury of going out to eat and sitting down at a restaurant and enjoying food with family. I also remember DC Mayor Muriel Bowser gave me a very nasty look at the grand opening. I'm not sure what happened prior to her arrival at Busboys and Poet's but I didn't need any of that energy.

Ward 8 Now Has a Sit-Down Restaurant: Busboys and Poets Welcomes the Community

It was a too good to be true two days ago on Tuesday, March 12, for the Ribbon Cutting Grand Opening of Busboys and Poets in Ward 8 at 2004 Martin Luther King Jr. Avenue in Southeast Washington, DC. "It's *been a long time coming,*" says Andy Shallal, owner of Busboys and Poets at the Ribbon Cutting Grand Opening. During his remarks, Shallal suggested using hashtag Ward 8 is great *#Ward8isgreat*, and we're going to make it even greater. As the owner, Shallal has plans to supplement, fortify, and not push out the other restaurants which were there before the red carpet arrived for the ribbon cutting. Mr. Shallal thanked the District Government for their support and efforts in ensuring the restaurant would open its doors. Andy stated how government is not necessarily the best friend of business, but business needs to be a part of the solutions. *"Get use to us,"* said Shallal at the ribbon cutting. Although he doesn't usually hear the word help very often, Andy Shallal was very proud to have been offered the help and support to open Busboys and Poets in Ward 8, even if he is somewhat speechless to call Far Southeast Family Strengthening Collaborative his landlords.

The project had been in development for the past 5 years. The full-service restaurant is on the ground floor of the new building. The Far Southeast Family Strengthening Collaborative made possible by Mayor Bowser\'s support including $3 million dollars in grants, and $8 million dollars in revenue bonds from the Office of the Deputy Mayor for Planning and Economic Development. An additional $2 million dollars was derived from the D.C.

Property Assessed Clean Energy (PACE) financing program administered by the D.C. Department of Energy and Environment and Urban Ingenuity according to the mayor's website. The total economic development investment was $13 million dollars for Busboys and Poets to open in Ward 8.

This innovative project builds on Mayor Bowser's ongoing commitment to expand prosperity and create pathways to the middle class for residents across all eight wards.

Many were in attendance for the celebration. *"Very excited because I'm a part of the board, it's a great day to have and bring this to Ward 8," says* Sandy Allen former Councilmember. The great Ward 8, the people can sit down, get culture, poetry, art, and the food is good, former Councilmember Sandy Allen added in support of the opening of Busboys and Poets. The restaurant resonates with the heart and soul of Ward 8 with the interior art adding ambiance and elegance along with the Marion Barry room to host events. The majority of the artwork featured in the Ward 8 Busboys and Poets are from Ward 8 and Commissioner Troy Donte' Prestwood thinks it's really special. Commissioner Prestwood suggests with recent headlines of gentrification, we have an opportunity to get it right. *"I hope people know the arrival of Busboys and Poets doesn't mean anyone is being forced out. Everyone is welcome to get a piece of the pie,"* he stated. Busboys and Poets is metro accessible. However, lunchtime parking is pretty congested, so perhaps parking around the perimeter of the restaurant and walking wouldn't be a bad idea, and you can work up an appetite for great food.

Title: Learn & Grow with Rooting DC

Interactive Source: YouTube.com

Original Production Year: ***2019***

<u>**MJ News Update:**</u> Capturing all the footage was really fun. What was most enjoyable was learning about all the plants and getting a bunch of seeds to test my green thumb. I really had a memorable time interviewing the people als

Rooting DC Is Building Healthy Communities

Do you recall the first time eating your fruits and vegetables? Or even better, do you remember the first seed that sprouted in a Styrofoam cup in your science class? Sure, you remember the first time you tasted some fresh collard greens, kale, spinach or squash. What about the time you received your first rose? Moreover, many are unaware of the process or ingredients involved with providing those fresh collards greens, kale, or spinach or the dozens of roses. Luckily, Rooting DC understands the importance of building healthy communities, by hosting a free all-day gardening forum that aims to provide education about urban food production, gardening, and food equity with the purpose of cultivating the health of our community and environment.

The love and enjoyment for agriculture in the district is evident. With over 700 people in attendance at Rooting DC on Saturday, February 23, there is no denying the delight for agriculture. Rooting DC was packed with much nutritional information, workshops, seed giveaways, sample foods, and a very strong building of an urban agriculture community. The event was held at Ron Brown College Preparatory High School.

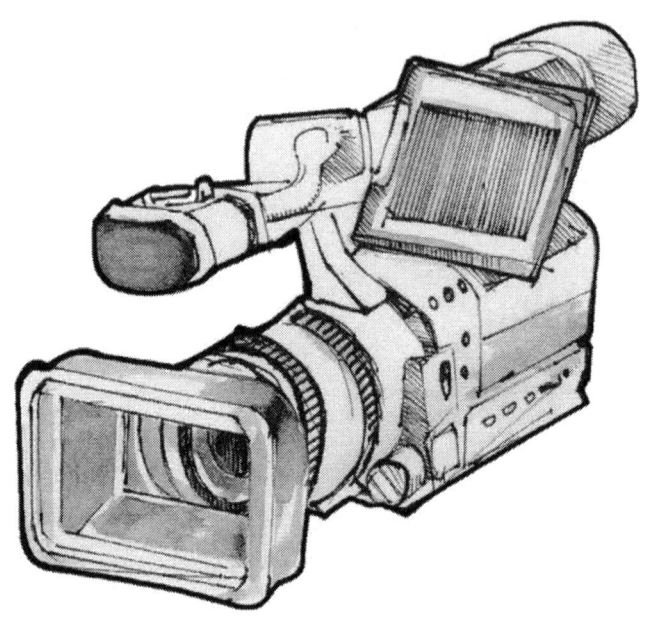

Title: North Michigan Park Community is ready for the Pax Liquor Protest Hearing

Interactive Source: Vimeo.com

Original Production Year: ***2019***

<u>***MJ News Update:***</u> Per my contractual obligation I was required to attend Advisory Neighborhood Commission meetings in Ward 5. That was a remarkable experience because I would really learn a more in-depth history about the neighborhood, and what their specific needs, and wants to sustain their

community. One thing I did learn very quickly is that they take as much pride in their community as they should. This was also a chance to learn which developers were coming to either enhance or encroach on the existing environment. It's also great to attend meetings where residents don't see you there, but they speak very highly of your work and want you at the meeting.

North Michigan Park Community is ready for the Pax Liquor Store Protest Hearing

Ahead of the City's Comprehensive Plan announcement, the North Michigan Park Community along with the Advisory Neighborhood Commission 5A are opposing the need for Pax Liquor Store in their community. The liquor store protest hearing is scheduled for *Wednesday, January 16*, 2019, and will be held at *2000 14th Street, NW* at **4:30 pm**

Title: North Michigan Park Community & ANC Oppose Pax Liquor by Protesting

Interactive Source: Vimeo.com

Original Production Year: ***2018***

MJ News Update: Some think of a liquor store as an opportunity zone, but that's until residents push back and that's just what Ward 5 residents did. They were very determined not to have another liquor store in their community. I appreciate showing up for the residents in their advocacy and protest efforts because they were victorious in their fight and no liquor store was in their community.

North Michigan Park Community and Advisory Neighborhood Commission Continue Protest Opposing Pax Liquor

North Michigan Park residents are furious and plan to protest about the influx of applications from non-DC residents seeking to open and operate liquor establishments in their community. This is the second alcohol license that the community has had to fight in the last six (6) months. ANC 5A successfully opposed the 4 Seasons Convenience Store Beer and Wine application, which ultimately was dismissed by the Alcohol Regulation Administration (ARBA) in August. Thereafter, a new liquor store application was filed by Pax Liquor, 4944 South Dakota Ave, N.E. and received by the

Commission. The protest is facilitated by ANC 5A and North Michigan Park Civic Association.

Ward 5 Residents Do Not Want 4 Seasons Selling Liquor on Sundays

A special meeting was called by the Advisory Neighborhood Commission 5A to address a critical concern. Reviewing the Alcoholic Beverage Control Board (ABRA) Application. This review process was critical because of the deadline, and its content; the final approved language 4 Seasons liquor license.

My note taking started on time, just when Chairman Edwards was reviewing proposed closing times for 4 Season Convenience store on Sundays. Although this is a special meeting for the ARBA Application finalization, none of the Ward 5 ANC Commissioners or community has ever met the owner of the liquor store. Moving right along with the meeting, it was now time to vote on the proposed closing hours for 4 Season Liquor store on Sundays. The proposed hours of operations were:

- *11 am – 6:30 pm*
- *noon- 6:00 pm*

Many were in favor of 4 Seasons Convenience store closing on Sundays. All in favor of closing counted **10** votes, **no constituents** were in favor of the proposed 11 am hours of operations. There were **2** constituents in favor of the liquor store opening at noon on Sundays. Although the vote had taken place, Commissioner Frank Wilds stated "opening on Sunday is up to owner's discretion, we can vote for it. "Even with the vote, ABRA still has the final authorization to approve hours of operation for the liquor store. Regardless of the decision, don't expect to purchase any single beer, only the pack according to Mr. Cho. He represented the liquor store on behalf of the owner who was on family vacation at the time when the community wanted to learn the need for the liquor store. However, the community insists 4 Seasons stays closed on Sundays. "It's worship Sunday, and they're open 6 days anyway," says Mr. Lockett. Someone stated that people purchase lottery tickets on Sunday, to which Mr. Lockett wasn't really feeling that expression,"I'm not standing for it," the liquor store being open on Sundays.

Parliamentarian, Grace Lewis was concerned that the constituents were imposing something on new owners and not imposing on other owners. With no plans for Plexi glass in the liquor store, some security concerns were raised. "Are the people going to have a gun in their store? They just can't go outside," says one constituent. According to Mr. Lockett, about five years ago, the owner of 4 Seasons came out with his shotgun for kids stealing. The ABRA Application and the Community Benefits Agreement are separate, furthermore the agreement still had a few more pages to flip through and read. " You're gone," Chairman Edwards asked Commissioner Frank Wilds as he turned over his nameplate and removed himself from the table. "Yes, I'm gone," he replied, and by that time it was 8:10 p.m. "We've been on this an hour and a half, stretching it a bit," suggested Chairman Edwards to the residents. Commissioner Lewis informed the constituents that they must bring justification forward for any opposition to which Mr. Lockett asked, "What about the 300 people?" Well, they sure were not at the Special Meeting to give more feedback to add when they initially signed opposing the liquor from the start. Vice-Chairman Gordon Fletcher stated that he gave a proper and timely notice. One resident was interested to learn "what do you call proper time?" It was obvious some of the residents received notice since they showed up to the Special Meeting. The Treasurer, Sandi Washington still had a few items on the agenda for further discussion and she suggested" we gotta bring this thing to a close." After flipping through the agreement with vigorous and intense debate, the ABRA Application Agreement was moved for the next phase of submission. Before closing the meeting, Sandi Washington presented the budget of $20,982.00 in the checking account and needed to get the residents to vote to buy out the copier machine or continue to lease it. The community agreed to buy out the copier machine with a maintenance plan. The meeting was finally adjourned a few minutes before 9.

Title: Washingtonian's Social Media Campaign Generate a Division in the District

Interactive Source: Vimeo.com

Original Production Year: ***2018***

<u>MJ News Update:</u> Being treated fairly isn't as universal as music, but most people are aware when they have said or done something offensive, especially any news outlets. Washingtonians weren't having any unfair treatment and came out in unison to protest the racial social media campaign.

Washingtonian's Social Media Campaign Generates a Division in the District

The District of Columbia, a dynamic city home to the capitol of the United States of America. It was once known as "Chocolate City," 200 years after President Lincoln signed the five-day delayed Declaration of Independence Proclamation, setting the slaves free. Despite the ongoing battle for "Statehood," the district has made some strides towards providing a sustainable lifestyle for its residents. However, many improvements can be added to the list of measurements for lifestyle benefits.

DC provides a space which cultivates opportunity that is tangible, however as of late many feels left out of the opportunities which hold value and impact their communities as a whole. Recently, the Washingtonian Magazine wanted to generate a buzz about the city using their social media Instagram account for the campaign push. Unfortunately, the social media campaign push got caught on the wrong hashtag line of **#ImNotATouristIliveHere**.

Taking into consideration that the Washingtonian has been DC's trusted local lifestyle resource for more than 50 years, and with this factored in, the Washingtonian has seen the drastic shift in lifestyles of District residents over the last 50 years. Most certainly their data reveals readership median income has increased to an estimated $230,000, and the average reader is 45 years of age. Many of the Washingtonian readers utilize the "Welcome Guide" as a first introduction into Washington, DC.

Perhaps many should adjust to this "new DC lifestyle." But what about those who have built the foundations for the city to transform at the current rate it is today to even consider a social media campaign? New is always good because it brings forth a feeling of change, but when an entire segment of the demographic of the city's population is not mentioned, does this distort the "Welcome Guide" into the city? Since the social media campaign didn't generate the commercial attraction, and displayed more of a divide among demographic data, the Washingtonian President and CEO, Catherine Merrill Williams has since issued a statement:

"This was the very beginning of a campaign in which all intentions are to include the many communities that make up our city. We solicited pictures from a diverse group of people and put the pictures up in the order they came in. People who saw the initial gallery of pictures had no way of knowing that it was not, in fact, the entirety of the marketing campaign. We took down the initial post because it created an impression that was inconsistent with our values and standards. We're confident that when the campaign is complete it will reflect the diversity of the readership that we serve."

Author, activist and social media influencer Tony Lewis, Jr. along with Angel Anderson added to the **#ImNotATouristILiveHere** social media campaign by organizing a **#DCNative** photo shoot. Surely from Sunday's turn out, it proved to be the missing demographic data of the population in the district. The **#DCNative** photo shoot took place at Union Market on May 20th. This particular location was meaningful and sent a message the event organizer thought. Union Market and surrounding areas in Ward 5 area has been the fastest and most developed region in the district.

The **#DCNative** movement comes at a monumental time since the Primary Elections are next month, June 19th.

'We Are a Community That Likes To Be Involved,' Health and Safety Are Concerns

The 5A Advisory Neighborhood Commission held their monthly meeting on Wednesday at Bernie Backus, UDC. Not sure if it's the topic on the agenda or more of an interest in community drawing the numbers, but it was well attended. This is like many developments are underway in Ward 5 such as Providence Hospital going through a vigorous name change and transition of patient care services. Add a spike in gun violence across the city, many residents want to ensure their community is cared for in an adequate and sustainable manner, but most of all safe.

Fourth District Commander Randy Griffin of the Metropolitan Police Department informed the community they are taking more of a holistic approach to address the crimes. Unfortunately, the community must understand gun violence isn't specifically a police problem according to Commander

Griffin, and more police don't solve the problem. Hopefully the holistic approach is the starting point for the solution. That way the community can see the plan of action being carried out. And since the streets south of Michigan Avenue are in the 5th District now, it is possible.

What currently has to be figured out is how Providence Healthcare will address the concerns of the community along with being able to provide the requested information to the 5A ANC Commissioners by the March 7th deadline. Representative Amha Selassie of the D.C. Department of Health presented some suggestions. However, had no plan of support in hand to give the Commissioners or share with the community? Mr. Selassie's suggestions were in support of Providence Hospital review of the Certificate of Need. Moreover, his purpose was to provide some clarity of the process, so Commissioner Washington was thankful he was present.

The Certificate of Need (CON), is the first permit that a healthcare provider needs before establishing a new service, facility, or before they provide the Letter of Intent, and before they spend $2.5 million dollars.

During the application review, the Certificate of Need must explain what they will be doing, what kind of patients they will have, and what services they will provide. One facet of the application requirement is that every applicant must inform the Neighborhood Advisory Commission. They sometimes receive input from the

Commissioners, however the Letter of Support (from the ANC) for the Certificate of Need is not required. The only rule is that they are informed. "And we want to be informed of the process," stated Chairman Edwards.

Commissioner Emily Singer Lucio was assuming Providence Hospital would notify them specifically of what the tone of their request is. "Absolutely," replied Mr. Selassie. That is the whole purpose. It serves two good purposes according to Mr. Selassie:

1) It gives the public a chance to know what is coming into their neighborhood.
2) It also notifies them of who is coming into their neighborhood.

Commissioner Washington was interested as to how they will know when the application is in. To which she learned, the applicant has to write a letter specifically to the Ward 5 ANC Commissioner. Commissioner Washington wanted further clarity on the Providence Hospital CON that expired last year, and if it can be transferred or if it covered the current request. Because of the new entity, Providence is providing a Health Village, along with provisional healthcare services including family medicine, internal medicine and geriatrics. The applicant of the Certificate of Need was present at the meeting, and did receive the support of the ANC Commission as long as Providence Health Services can provide the following:

1) Commission sees the application
2) Commission would like to see the Letter of Support from the other ANCs
3) Provide a confirmation to the Commission they have spoken to Councilmember McDuffie

Moreover, the Commissioners want to avoid any appearance of a workaround process for the Certificate of Need. A decrease in services was the reason for Providence

Hospital's closure. The curtailment of service does not align with the needs of the community.

The meeting was adjourned around 9:02 pm.

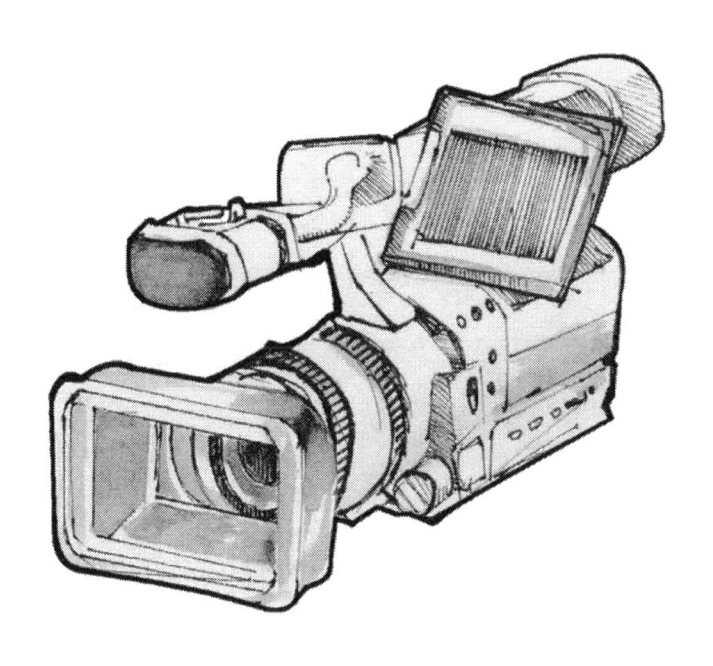

Title: H Street Festival, Family, Friends, & Much Fun

Interactive Source: YouTube.com

Original Production Year: ***2019***

MJ News Update: Attending a festival in the city is always a wonderful time. This affords the opportunity to reach new readers and reconnect with people you haven't seen in a while. Festival time also brings all the merchants out and you can purchase some really cool items.

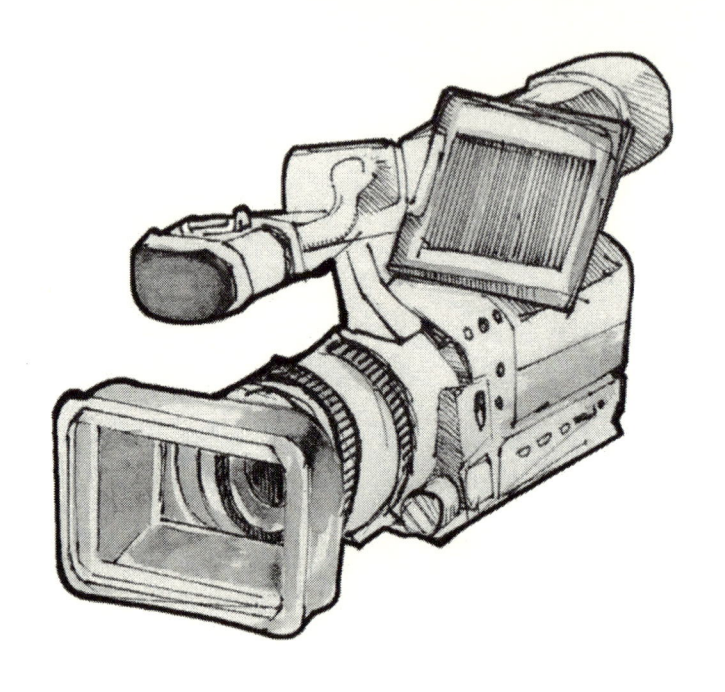

Title: The Cannabis Climate in the District
Interactive Source: YouTube.com

Original Production Year: *2017*

MJ News Update: Mary Jane is what they called marijuana at one point, but it has arrived at Cannabis now, and that's the way consumers can purchase it in the city. Because of initiative 71, residents were able to partake in a toke session with adults only. I initially reported on this bill passing when it first became law and residents were pleased to have something they can agree on even if some are not interested in a smoke session.

The Cannabis Climate in the District

It was a cold and brisk night in the District on February 27, 2015, when Mayor Muriel Bowser announced the legalization of marijuana for recreational and medical use. How fitting to complement the overwhelming vote of *Yes* for initiative 71; it just sticks together like RAW papers. One year later, the flowers are budding across the city and most certainly at Capital City Care, one of the premier medical marijuana dispensaries in the district. We had the opportunity for an exclusive one-on-one interview with Maishah Asante-English, Community Outreach and Marketing Coordinator early on a Thursday morning, just a few hours before any patients would arrive for care. Have you ever wondered what in the clouds does it look like at a medical marijuana dispensary in the district? Well, here it is. Enjoy our exclusive conversation with Capital City Care.

With there being so much focus on companies generating revenue in the industry the care of the patient can go unnoticed, so how are patients feeling about Capital City Care?

We have had numerous patients tell us how much they enjoy the atmosphere in the dispensary. We really try to treat patients as if they were friends or family and want everyone to feel comfortable from the moment they walk in the door. Personal attention is one of our main goals and we want each patient to feel like a VIP. They have been excited about our increased supply and lower prices. They are all eager to try out the variety of new strains that have been appearing in recent months.

Do all of your patients receive a consultation?

At Capital City, we take pride in ensuring first-time patients are properly educated on the medical marijuana program here in the district and the specifics of our dispensary. Whether the patient has had experience with medical cannabis or not, all of our staff take time to walk new patients through the process, discussing details of our product and pairing patients with what may be the best option for their specific needs.

What is the maximum amount of medicinal marijuana a patient can receive on their visit at Capital City Care?

Medical marijuana patients in the District are allowed to purchase up to 2 ounces (or 56 grams) of our products, which includes flower, hash, tinctures, and oil cartridges in a 30-day period. An additional 56 grams can be purchased with physician approval as long as this purchase does not include flower.

If a patient has the allowable grams and supply is available, they are welcome to purchase the maximum allowed. Now that we have increased our quantities, we are now seeing more patients by 1/2 ounces and ounces in one visit.

If Capital City Care were a flower, what would be the name and which strain would it be an indica, sativa, or hybrid?

I would definitely vote for hybrid and think Blue Dream would be the best name pick since we are relaxed but focused. Our staff all come from a variety of backgrounds and offer a nice blend of experience with cannabis, fun personalities and sincere care for our patients.

How many jobs has Capital City Care provided?

As the District\'s medical marijuana program has expanded in 2 years, we have had to increase our staff to accommodate the growing number of patients. We started out with just two people (our owners), who did everything when we opened and now have a staff of 7.

Do your patients have to be DC residents?

Yes, the Department of Health does require that all medical marijuana patients live in the District of Columbia and provide proof of residency. We're always available if patients have questions about the requirements.

Did Capital City Care face any challenges opening up in the community? How long did it take to open your doors once the law was in effect?

Starting a new business is never easy, especially with the strict regulations we operate under. Fortunately, support for medical marijuana has been strong in the district for a long time now and it felt as though everyone wanted to make the program a success. The Dept. of Health, the Metropolitan

Police Department and the D.C. Council all played important roles in helping make this possible.

Is there a cost associated with obtaining a medical marijuana card? If so, how much?

The application fee is $100 or $25 for low-income patients. There can be additional costs if the patient needs to see a new doctor in order to get approved. We often help patients find the best available options and we offer generous new patient specials to help make the process more affordable.

Although patients can grow, do you still find that patients still choose Capital City Care?

A number of patients are now taking advantage of the District's law allowing them to grow. However, those same patients continue to purchase products here at Capital City Care for a number of reasons. Some rely on the quality of the product that they have become familiar with. Others might find their own plants were not as potent as they expected. Many have told me they will continue to purchase specific products from us, such as oils, tinctures, and hash, that they are not interested in attempting on their own.

What would a gram cost on average?

Capital City Care has the best prices in the District, with no gram costing more than $20 and great selections available at $16 and $18.

Are the conditions for the use of medicinal marijuana vary from patient to patient?

Patients come in the door with a variety of conditions, from diabetes and fibromyalgia to cancer and glaucoma. During our initial consultation with patients, we work to find the best strain to address their specific needs.

One last question before we have to go because you all have to get ready to open for patients, if people are interested in alternative medicine options can they contact Capital City Care?

Absolutely. We're always happy to hear from prospective patients. We've helped many people navigate the application process and get their medical marijuana cared. It's not as difficult as it sounds, and there's never been a better time to do it.

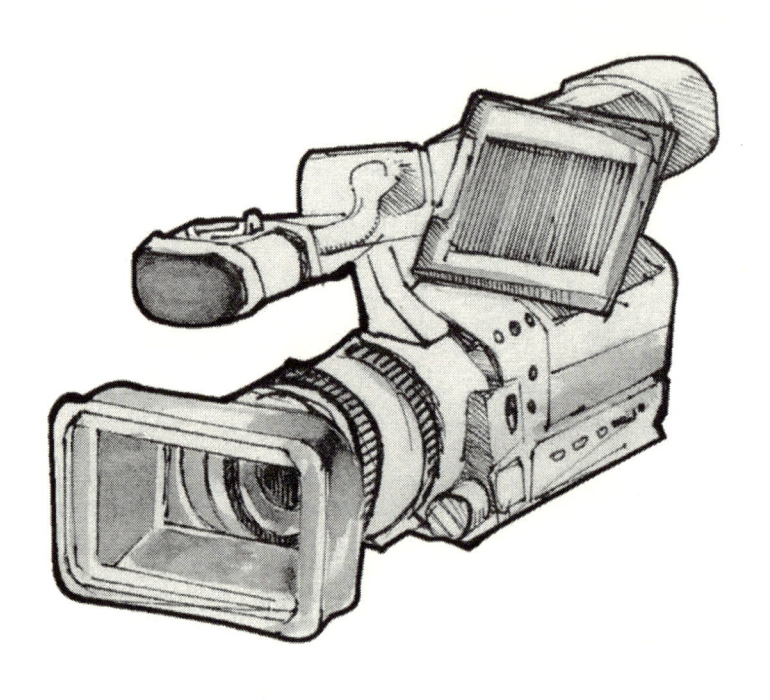

Title: Donald Trump Jr. brings the heat to Washington with the NRA

Interactive Source: YouTube.com

Original Production Year: *2016*

MJ News Update: Being at the right place at the right time is how I can express this particular opportunity. I was just hanging out in a restaurant near Capitol Hill, enjoying some chips and salsa, then I saw a few reporters that I recognized and thought something was about to happen, and it sure was. I was very glad to get the story first-hand.

Donald Trump, Jr. Brings the Heat to Washington with the NRA

After about 40 days of rain, our nation's capital has finally seen the sunshine, and in fact it was a blazing 94 degrees. As if Wednesday wasn't hot enough in Washington, Donald Trump Jr. had a meet and greet with Rep. Chris Collins (R-NY) at the National Rifle

Association (NRA); a Chris Cox sponsored gathering along with some 15 other House

Republicans eager to meet the son of the Republican Presidential contender Donald Trump. This meet and greet comes a week after the NRA endorsed Donald Trump for President of the US. The DC Voice asked Rep. Collins how the NRA arrived at the ultimate decision to endorse Trump. Tune in now…

Title: Mentors making a difference in the Metro City

Interactive Source: YouTube.com
Original Production Year: ***2016***

MJ News Update: Having a mentor can make a major difference in your life.

Everyone needs someone to talk to even if it's just to express an idea or feelings. There are many benefits to having a mentor and it can improve your lifestyle tremendously. Most successful people have had some form of guidance outside of the home to help them mature in their craft.

Mentors Making a Difference in the Metro City

Growing up in the nation's capital had its moments, and challenges, but DC is the city where only the strong survive; and those skills were often applied on a daily basis. Although many opportunities and resources were available, some children still wanted to find trouble. Others wanted alternative after-school outlets other than getting caught up in trouble. Luckily, for Deon he had track as his alternative after school, which lead him to the boxing arena.

If you were not aware, the boxing scene in the District has always been buzzing, and busy before Adrien Broner arrived on April 1. I remember my brother being an extra for a Mike Tyson and Don King commercial back in the 90's. Moreover, DC no longer has that 90's flavor, but the 90's was when "Tiny" had his last fight in Atlantic city.

Mr. Mcintyre is a former undefeated amateur and professional champion coming out of Fenley's boxing gym located in the north-east quadrant of the city. He wanted inner city youth to have the same opportunity, which was presented to him, so he started training youth outside without a gym just to get them away from crime and challenges of living in the inner city. True champions aim to achieve goals, and Deon says, "my goal is to find a boxing home for me to continue to train them to become champions and not victims of the streets." Mr. Mcintyre is doing the best he can with the limited resources that he has, however he plans to continue providing a positive outlet for inner city youth with hopes for some future government support.

Title: P.A.I.N.T.S. Covers the District

Interactive Source: YouTube.com

Original Production Year: **2016**

MJ News Update: Art is very inspiring and holds value not only to the artist but for the collective especially if the work was commissioned by another. It adds some color, style, even grace to any space and makes you feel good about contributing your work on a whole new level.

P.A.I.N.T.S Covers the District

Take a second just to think "what would our world be without ART?" Sure the thought was very stale, boring, not much culture nor creativity. Luckily The P.A.I.N.T.S. Institute knows the impact and importance ART places in our society, and throughout the world. It was demonstrated at the Howard Theater for the unveiling of the masterpiece "DC Wards Story Collection." Scrolling our Instagram feed we stopped on P.A.I.N.T.S. page with its beautiful art and bright colors. Furthermore, we made the invite list to bring you this phenomenal program initiative. The 2016 Art Leadership Program is a holistic summer internship that focuses on art education in the context of the whole person by combining both academic and technical instruction in various artistic mediums with experiential learning opportunities, and much more.

DC Wards Story Collection

The 2016 intern class boasts 19 of the most creative D.C. youth between the ages of 14 and
24. The class is led by a cadre of six young adults. Without a doubt, "DC Wards Story Collection" inspired the crowd. The

creators and the city are in for a great treat. Briefly speaking with Executive Director, John Chisholm, we learned that this is a six weeks leadership program held at the University of the District of Columbia. That was enough for us. The program participants had the opportunity to work alongside Creative Director, Demont *"Peekaso"* Pinder. While creating "DC Wards Story Collection" Mr. Pinder says "the beauty of this whole project is to show what happens when you come together as one and create something."

The 2016 Aspiring Artists are:
Adelaide Mendelson   Dej' anelle "PHRANC" Grimes   Kemonie Carter   Nidia Leak

Alston Tobin   Irving Silva   Maurice Ogletree   Sanika Williams   Yasmine Posey

Christopher Ackerman   Jillian Jackson   Melvin West   Simone Crozier   Tray Johnson

D\'Angelo Martino   Janae Charles   Matthew McLean   Stephanie Berry   Taijhona Smith

Title: *The Panel Discussion*

Interactive Source: YouTube.com

Original Production Year: ***2016***

<u>**MJ News Update**</u>: Being able to attend panel discussions are always rewarding. Either way you learn something knew which adds value and meaning. Panel discussions also provide an opportunity to ask questions and gain more insight on topics that interest you. Always be ready to listen and then speak to and share when attending a discussion.

THE PANEL DISCUSSION

Some would agree to disagree that the melody makes the music sound great. On the other hand, it's the lyrics which complement the melody make the music sound great. While others would agree Hip Hop derived from up-top, New York, and call-and-response, a great form of independent expression came from New Orleans. Well, when you fuse Jazz and Wu-Tang influenced Hip Hop, it sparks the soothing soul sounds of SHAOLIN Jazz. Those keys and the arrangement of the melody on the 37th Chamber 'Mighty Meth' certainly keeps it moving, and The PANEL DISCUSSION which took place at Busboys and Poets keep the conversation moving with SHAOLIN Jazz sharing their recent visit to Addis Ababa, Ethiopia.

Music is most definitely a universal language infused with culture, along with a wide range of dialects which speaks to the soul evoking the raw sound delivering rhymes and improvisation. Grammy-nominated Ethiopian American vocalist Wayna says this of the ability to freestyle "it sort of a spiritual and biological connection." Her education came as an artist since she lived in the suburbs away from the environment to foster that creativity. Given the right tools and environment it can come out, she says that of the ability to create a song with freestyle in particular. With the influence of Eric Roberson, she gained the knowledge and understanding to make up a song about the people in the audience at a show, or what\'s going on in the news.

The PANEL DISCUSSION also included the creators of SHAOLIN Jazz, Gerald Watson who grew up with the sounds of Jazz, and DJ 2-Tone Jones whose deep connection to drums and percussion can surely be heard in the 37th Chamber. Professor and award-winning filmmaker Tewodross Melchishua shared his Jazz influences and knowledge he teaches his students at Bowie University. The PANEL DISCUSSION was moderated by Keanna Faircloth host of 'Evening Jazz' on WPFW 89.3fm. A great discussion and shared experience infused with Jazz and Hip Hop which creates the sound of SHAOLIN Jazz.

Title: *Affordable and Healthy Living, The Wren*

Interactive Source: Vimeo.com

Original Production Year: **2017**

MJ News Update: Access to affordable housing has been a challenge not just in the district but across the United States. However, in Washington, it's like finding a needle in a haystack. The DC City Council couldn't tell you when the last time affordable housing was even applicable or granted to residents. Every inch of the city now has a new development structure that isn't affordable.

What's New, Affordable, and Healthy Living? The Wren

Today was the groundbreaking ceremony for The Wren, a new in the Shaw neighborhood expected for occupancy by July 2020 with development efforts by MRP Reality , Ellis Development, and JBG Smith.

The Wren is most certainly what Washingtonian's need right now! Something new and affordable to come home to after a longs day of work. "I'm a native Washingtonian, and lifetime resident of the Shaw neighborhood, and glad to see it where it is. It will enhance Shaw. Affordable housing is good, along with Whole Foods Market to bring nutrition to the community is good, since this area has been vacated so long," says Gretchen Wharton, Chair of Shaw Main Streets.

Residents in the Shaw neighborhood have much to look forward when The Wren is ready for occupancy in 2020. Beginning with 30% of their units being affordable, metro accessible, walking distance to DC's hottest nightlife, entertainment, and restaurants. Whole Foods Market will only plan to occupy 46,000 sq. feet of the street level retail space. The project plans to provide over $500 thousand dollars to support local hiring, business, and entrepreneurship. The developers also plan on improving the intersection, travel lanes, sidewalks, and streetscape along Sherman Ave.

Although the application process for the 433-unit development has not started, residents will soon be able to get more information about The Wren from MRP Reality.

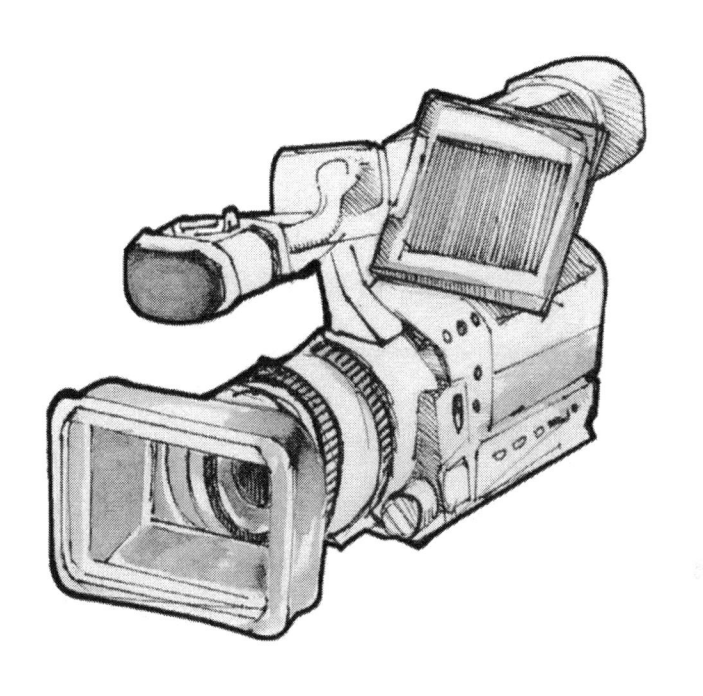

Title: DC Mayor for Life Marion Barry Legacy Lives On

Interactive Source: YouTube.com

Original Production Year: *2018*

MJ News Update: When I grew up in DC, Marion Barry was the Mayor. I do remember that many people in the city were flourishing, especially the Black People. You could always see someone reading a newspaper, and the Youth Employment Program started during his administration.

The Legacy of Marion Barry, Jr. Lives on in the District

The District is 3 months away from the primary elections, which registered voters can elect a new Mayor, along with other governing officials. No matter the outcome, it is sort of set in stone that Marion S. Barry, Jr. is DC's Mayor for life.

After arriving in Washington in 1965 to lead the SNCC office, Marion Barry, Jr. believed that the public safety employees should reflect in the community. During January of 1978, Marion Barry kicked off his official campaign for Mayor of the District of Columbia. He was the second Mayor ever elected in DC, serving 3 terms until 1990 and has been the honorable Mayor for life ever since. Even while serving as Councilmember, he was still Mayor for life. "Always fighting for the people," Marion Barry devoted over 40 years of his life to public service until his untimely death in November 2014.

On Saturday, March 3, Mayor Muriel Bowser along with many others recognized Marion

Barry. Dedicating an eight-foot bronze statue sculpted by artist Steven Weitzman of Weitzman Studios. The statue is in the likeness of 4-term Mayor of Washington, DC, Marion Barry, Jr.

Title: Ward 5 Hidden Treasures

Interactive Source: YouTube.com

Original Production Year: **2016**

MJ News Update: When it comes to fashion and the district it's a fuse like no other! You can't tell anyone in the district they don't have any fashion sense, a fight can start fast. I have learned to embrace all facets of fashion because I'm no designer, but I do know how to put a few pieces together if need be.

Ward 5 Hidden Treasures

Being the largest ward in the District, it's possible that some Ward 5 hidden treasures can go unnoticed. However, luckily for one captivating, cozy, cultured, and vibrant venue; The Museum, residents and creators alike can make their visions come to life. Located at 2014 Rhode Island Avenue, not too far from the printing shop you won't miss The Museum. Although the event was RSVP, the doors of The Museum were open for fashion lovers, models, artists, designers, and pairing all this with a classic Reebok makes for a perfect blend of styles.

Redline Transit Hat Debut

The Museum is founded by "G" The Future Mogul, and he encourages all creators to bring their creative ideas down to The Museum. Many celebrities were at The Museum awaiting the debut of the "Redline transit" hat along with other clothing apparel for purchase. We had the opportunity to meet various artist and designers who are taking the

District to new heights. If you are in the area, or not in the area, just be sure to add The Museum to your "to do" list. You don't want to miss this marvelous museum.

Chapter Two: POLITICS

Should the United States Foot the Bill to Rebuild Venezuela if the United Nations Failed to Act?

This is an important question which requires some critical decision making and involves much logistics and coordination at federal levels. The starting point could possibly be to exam the Declaration of Independence and the United States Constitution. Considering Congress adopted the Declaration of Independence on July 4, 1776, publicly announced to the world the unanimous decision of the American colonies to declare themselves free and independent states, absolved from any allegiance to Great Britain. What is a humanitarian crisis and how fast should the United States respond?

To further assist with answering the critical question, a great next step can be to define humanitarian and crisis. Once defined compare and contrast the crisis at hand currently to past humanitarian crisis on US soil and if the US could afford to give its support, along with being able to provide the same scale and support to its own citizens. What does that data reveal and how can it improve the current concerns of Venezuela? A humanitarian is a person promoting human welfare and social reform, a philanthropist, according to Webster Dictionary. A crisis is a turning point or critical situation, and together Venezuela needs help with a critical situation to provide social reform.

Should this critical decision be solely the responsibility of the United States alone? Why do other countries always look to the United States as the primary subsidizer to bail them out of disastrous situations? Suppose this is where understanding of compassion and empathy for humanity can be factored into the equation. Humanity is defined by the quality or state of being human. This is wonderful to know especially since the need to be anything else serves limited purpose because being human exceeds all.

Now we should factor in the agency or organization that will be responsible for implementation of logistics and coordination efforts with social service agencies with boots on the grounds. We must also consider the jurisdiction power and authority the United States will be granted if providing the aid in an effort to rebuild Venezuela. From past natural disasters on American soil such as Hurricane Katrina, in which the levees breached in the lower 9th Ward washing away most of the structures in land, while displacing millions of the native residents. Hurricane Katrina was over 13 years ago and the recovery efforts can still use some community engagement efforts. The economy is always the first caveat to consider when rebuilding, and New Orleans Louisiana leads number one in Hospitality and Tourism in the United States. Not to mention the extraordinary cuisine and culture. If the people are what enrich a city's culture ensuring it can thrive and prosper, should the United States continue to focus on providing and combating the housing humanitarian crisis currently in New Orleans and across America.

Recently, NYU held a symposium "Outlook on Venezuela, The Roadmap to Recovery," to which distinguished experts and international leaders to discuss the crisis in Venezuela, as well as the next steps in rebuilding the country's economy, infrastructure, and institutions. Opposition leaders within the country and international community are looking ahead to a democratic transition of power while at the same time focusing on the reconstruction of Venezuela's economy. According to Michael Shiffer, President of Inter-American Dialogue suggest crossing that river has been the hardest task, while preventing ships from docking in Miami have been enforced. Shiffer suggests "there is always a hope for change," and back in January he joined in the hope however they got it wrong and hard to know what the crystal ball will reveal.

The primary organization who will have a vital role in this recovery effort if the United States plans to participate would be Organizations of America. OAS is a continental organization that was founded on April 30, 1948, for the purposes of regional solidarity and cooperation among its member states. Members are the 35 independent states of Americas lead by Secretary General Luis Almagro Lemes. A common thread expressed among the distinguished panelist was getting rid of the old regime in Venezuela for the United States to encourage and not lead the path to pointless dialogue, regarding sanctions, political support and economic support and how are these facets being managed. In terms of political support, no parties responded, and the military groups have been infiltrated with thugs causing a divide under the current regime. What have those results shown and does data reveal the ability for a government to governing the living standard of the people?

Currently, India is the largest 3rd party application of sanctions purchaser of Venezuela oil which is becoming more and more dangerous magnifying the criminal economy in Venezuela. Venezuela proposed a financial sanction Emergency Order which deals with the threat to US characterization of the sanctions. The authority to allow sanctions is designed by Congress, and currently Russian oil companies are commercializing Venezuela oil without violating United States sanctions. This could be a potential model approach going forward. OAS Secretary General is taking issues on for Venezuela, however certain limits to what OAS can do to play an important role to which an ambassador can help with the transition providing sustainable solutions.

What can an ambassador do? They can help with galvanizing support needed for engagement efforts along with boosting the voting moral of the people in rural areas of their member representation. The right to vote is critical not just in Venezuela, but

Indonesia and in the United States of America where much discussion of getting rid of the

Electoral College vote has generated buzz. If one of the members of OAS obstructs the voting process within the jurisdiction of the United States of America with specific regards to Washington, DC should that member's representation be revoked? In this particular case should Trinidad and Tobago be evaluated in their role of obstructing the United States Constitution to support major technology companies such as Alphabet\'s subsidiary company Google Incorporation?

MJ News Update: Distractions are very real. And many were coming my way during the time I wrote this article, April 2019. This would be the last article I wrote for the DC Voice online news publication. I can recall attending the symposium at NY University DC campus and going to a fancy restaurant after the event to start writing the article. It took me a few days to write it, and it was worth it in the end. The article was eventually retweeted on the Twitter social media platform by the moderator of the discussion so that was outstanding. Moreover, currently in the United States Colorado has been reporting how Venezuela gang members are taking over apartment buildings and collecting rent from the tenants.

Title: The Second Time around Mayor Bowser's Fair Shot February

Interactive Source: YouTube.com

Original Production Year: ***2019***

MJ News Update: I was pleasantly surprised to learn that DC Mayor Bowser would be holding her Fair shot discussion at Gallaudet University for many reasons. I wasn't sure if this was because she was trying to support her friends during a Google litigation process, or because she wanted to generate a buzz for the learning institution. Meanwhile, it was very embarrassing to see that the number of jobs her administration informed the public about was inaccurate. It just speaks volumes of how much went wrong under her watch.

Mayor Bowser Promises a Fair Shot February

Mayor Muriel Bowser held her two term outlook at Gallaudet University lead by various panel discussions to highlight the progress made in the district. This is certainly a new approach and strategy to present investing in DC values, providing affordable housing, a more inclusive city, and most importantly a way to show accountability throughout the entire District Government agencies. Mayor Bowser\'s second time around just may be the charm for the constituents of the District of Columbia.

The Executive Summary Report presented by the Office of the Mayor had vibrant colors on the page, and what popped out the most was the accurate number of jobs created in the district. Is it 800, 80,000, or 800,000? Former Mayor Anthony Williams was in attendance to reflect on his term as Mayor and congratulate Mayor Bowser on her second time around along with the progress she has made turning the city around providing many investment opportunities and bring a better quality of life for the residents in the city.

Those in attendance had the opportunity to hear from various government agencies and learn about the work they are doing for residents to keep the city thriving and keeping DC Values first. Residents will have an opportunity to take advantage of the offerings during Mayor Bowser\'s Fair Shot February which kicks off today at the Wilson Building. Be sure to get your Fair Shot, follow the great finding happening throughout the month:

- February 4, at 5:00 pm – Wilson Building Open House
- February 5, 7:00 pm – Congressional Reception
- February 11, 12:00 pm – Senior Telephone Townhall
- February 21, 6:30 pm – Budget Engagement Forum (Arthur Capper Community Center)
- February 23, 10:00 am – Budget Engagement Forum (Deanwood Recreation Center)
- February 25, 6:30 pm – Budget Engagement Forum (Roosevelt High School)

Title: Race & Policy: Advancing Racial Equity, & Economic Inclusion in DC

Interactive Source: YouTube.com

Original Production Year: *2019*

MJ News Update: I recall this conversation for several reason and one being how crowded the room was and people had to watch and listen from across the hall. The resident's showed up and had many questions for those in charge of the school system in the District. Not sure how time ran out but Councilmember McDuffie should have held a continuation of the conversation.

A Critical Conversation Continues Beyond the Symposium: Education in the District of Columbia

R.I.S.E. Demonstration Center was the place to be for the *"Race & Policy: Advancing Racial Equity and Economic Inclusion in the District of Columbia"* symposium co-hosted by Councilmember Kenyan McDuffie along with the D.C. Policy Center and Consumer Health Foundation.

The well-attended event was standing room only, awaiting the panel discussions on various topics to take place:

- Education & Employment – Achieving Racial Equity in District of Columbia Education
- Health – Examining the Determinants of Health Equity
- Housing & Economic Development – Revitalizing Communities to Achieve Racial Equity
- Access to Capital for Minority – Owned Small Business in DC

In time for the very heated and engaged *Education & Employment – Achieving Racial Equity in District of Columbia Education* panel discussion, moderated by Kristen Moore, Ed.D., Coordinator, Student Empowerment and Equity Programs, some in attendance felt there wasn't enough time for presenting more than three questions, on such critical issues currently impacting students in the public schools. Councilmember McDuffie stood at the podium in the crowded room at the R.I.S.E. Demonstration Center and informed all attendees that the symposium wouldn't be the last and due to the responses the conversation should continue at a later time considering three other panels were scheduled to present.

Currently, the city's education system is going through a transition from the selection of a school Chancellor to learning which curriculum works best in this digital age while keeping students engaged in the classroom lessons. Not only the transition underway, but the past history of inflation of test scores, school books staying in the warehouse instead of at the schools, low graduation rates, along with students dying on school premises. Perhaps, continuing the conversation is vital and critical to maintaining any possibility of change in the District Public School system, and looks to be Councilmember McDuffie is leading the charge with providing a safe space for a panel discussion despite only three questions being presented by the audience.

The conversation is to be continued and here are a few questions that could spark that conversation:

- How do we educate families?
- What does it mean to prepare students and families for education?
- How do you close the achievement gap when a student's confidence is lost?
- How will students with impoverished backgrounds cover the cost of college textbooks?

Title: 157th Emancipation Day Celebration in DC: What does freedom mean to you?

Interactive Source: YouTube.com

Original Production Year: *2019*

MJ News Update: If you didn't stand upright for it what makes you assume you're deserving of it? Freedom, what many take for granted but what is it? Most people associate it with a time period of slavery and is often associated with such, so how do you define it and apply it in the 21st century if you're not fighting for it, or maybe you don't feel the need to fight for it.

What Does Freedom Mean During the 157th Emancipation Day Celebration?

What's one word we seldom think of, often take for granted, and servicemen and women must protect at all costs to be offered to every citizen of this great nation America? **Freedom** is the word. According to Webster's Seventh New Collegiate Dictionary, **Freedom** means the quality or state of being free as action, or a political right. Although the meaning appears straight-forward, not many in America were fond of granting freedom to all citizens. The district celebrated the 157th Emancipation Day on April 13, 2018. Mayor Bowser, along with community organizations and Administration officials will march to increase awareness around the district's progress in advancing civil rights and achieving full democracy through statehood.

It wasn't until 1862 with a responsible 5-day delay, where President Abraham Lincoln felt in his heart to grant slaves in the District of Columbia the rights as normal citizens. That courageous and heart felt act of human compassion and kindness has led to the Emancipation Proclamation freeing slaves in the Confederate states. Which later opened up the opportunity to serve as an American serviceman. Whether freedom was equal to all existing citizens and former slaves among the laws of the land that governed America, would be the ultimate test of the nation's fabric.

Freedom is a simple word, but very profound and hold much meaning for American citizens. Because of the United States Constitution, citizens of the America have certain unalienable rights granted by their creator, and the 1st Amendment to the United States Constitution is what grants American citizens the right to be free, starting with expression. So, what does Freedom mean to you during this 157th Emancipation Day celebration in the district?

Title: Sexual Harassment and Misconduct

Interactive Source: Vimeo.com

Original Production Year: ***2018***

<u>MJ News Update:</u> The weather was very strange this day. A light sheet of snow had fallen covering the trees and ground. Despite the conditions I couldn't miss this hearing because I had to interview a few farmers. This would also be the last time I would see Congressman Elijah Cummings in good health at a Congressional hearing.

Sexual Harassment and Misconduct are Societal Issues or Issues Concerning Many Government Agencies Starting with USDA then the Forest

From the Hollywood Hills to Silicon Valley, in the fields of USDA, through the U.S. Forest Services; sexual harassment and misconduct have become a societal problem not a systemic problem within corporations, according to Sundar Pichai, Google CEO. That could be examined from a binary lens view. Viewing from the on switch, sexual harassment and misconduct could be a societal issue. However, viewing from the off switch, recognizing the signs and concerns of sexual harassment could be systematic within government agencies and corporations. Regardless of a binary view, the

Full House Committee on Oversight and Government Reform held a hearing on November 15, 2018, to examine the U.S. Forest Service\'s response to allegations of misconduct, sexual harassment, discrimination, and retaliation.

Prior to November 15, 2018, the Committee held a hearing on December 1, 2016 to examine reported misconduct, harassment, and gender discrimination at the U.S. Department of Agriculture (USDA) and the U.S. Forest Service (USFS). Despite the initiatives launched to improve the work environment, the reports of misconduct, retaliation, and sexual harassment continue. The USDA Office of the Inspector General (OIG) issued an interim audit report as of March 18, 2018, and are preparing a full audit report to determine whether USFS\'s actions to address complaints were implemented in accordance with USFS\'s agreement with the Office of the General Counsel and the Office of the Assistant Secretary for Civil Rights.

The witnesses and testimonies panel for the recently held hearing included Ms. Vicki

Christiansen, Chief of U.S. Forest Service, The Honorable Phyllis K. Fong, Inspector General

U.S. Department of Agriculture, and Ms. Shannon Reed former Air Quality Specialist at the U.S. Forest Service. In Ms. Reed's case, it could be examined from the binary off switch view – recognizing the signs and concerns of sexual harassment within a government agency. Ms. Reed was supported by the *USDA Coalition of Minority Employees* along with others during her testimony. She started off in Forest Services and was touched by a Supervisor. That touch then leads to an improper personal relationship resulting in Ms. Reed refusing her supervisors advances. Once Ms. Reed filed a complaint to report the improper advances, she was suspended for 7 days. However, she was rated fully successful in her performance appraisal for the years 2015-17. During her testimony, Ms. Reed expressed that she believes her suspension was because she had reported the improper advances.

Ms. Reed believed that Park Services would give her a fresh start and a new outlook on life, but she felt like "jumping from the frying pan, into the fire." Ranking Member Elijah Cummings expressed to Ms. Reed "I'm sorry that you have had to make so many moves to try and find a safe place to work, in 2018." Congressman Cummings stated it shouldn't be tolerated by this government or any other workplace. "What would make this right?," Ranking Member asked Ms. Reed. She believes the Park Service should fire the perpetrators and rid that agency of those perpetrators and those predators. Surprisingly, Ms.

Christiansen, Chief of U.S. Forest Services had some feedback for Congressman Elijah Cummings. "I absolutely agree. I can assure you that every allegation has a full investigation. The harassment risk, HART team takes the minor bullying and non-sexual cases, and they do an inquiry. Anything that is sexual harassment goes through a full certified investigation. Now, it is possible the information from the investigation will be redacted showing how the agency manages critical concerns before scheduled Committee hearings. Furthermore, Ms. Christiansen was unable to make any comments about any specific cases, but is committed to changing the culture.

Chief Christiansen expressed to the Committee "I would like to say I could change it in 6 months." She should share her culture cleanup codes with those in Silicon Valley, on and the movie sets of Hollywood, but this issue could be examined from a binary view, a societal issue. Furthermore, Chief Christiansen said "to be absolutely honest, I don't think you can change a culture of an organization that's existed for 113 years, has 40,000 people that has a mission of getting critical jobs done in remote locations overnight." That could very well be a borderline excuse with not much enthusiasm or optimism to see the culture shift. Ms. Christiansen agreed to work with pace to change parts of the culture the agency sees as important. She informed the Committee that it was a possibility that they were speaking of two different things about culture, and you just don't legislate culture. Chief Christiansen asked the Committee for additional suggestions for help, and she is all ears.

The behavior of sexual harassment and misconduct along with retaliation are not OK, and Ms. Christiansen stressed to the Committee that on behalf of the 40,000 employees, will establish a code of conduct, but she did inform them just like any life population, there are people that are not doing the right thing. They do not respect each other and that is not OK. "I think they are hearing the message today from all of us on the witness panel that this is a zero-tolerance situation and that we stand ready to assist people who have concerns," Chief Christiansen assured Congress.

Title: Young Black Leadership Summit State of the Union Address

Interactive Source: YouTube.com

Original Production Year: ***2018***

<u>***MJ News Update:***</u> The power of social media can be very rewarding. This opportunity was presented to me by one of my supporters on Instagram. One of my supporters suggested that I attend Turning Point USA event, and I was granted the opportunity. I appreciate when people see your talents and take you serious and something spectacular comes out and it did in this content.

BLEXIT is Makes a Bold Statement by Breaking the Bondage of Political Orthodoxy in America

The recent launch of the *BLEXIT* movement was announced on October 27th by Candace Ownens, TPUSA Communications Director, during the Young Black Leadership Summit held in Washington, DC. What is *BLEXIT*? A frequency for those who have released themselves from political orthodoxy, fueled by individuals choosing freedom over tyranny. *BLEXIT* is about the individual journeys of free thinkers across the country connected by a vision and the values we hold dear. Tune in to watch the launch of

B: **Family**   *L:* **Culture**   *E:* **Belief**   *X:* **Freedom**   *I:* **Progress**   *X:* **Strength**

Title: Young Black Leadership Summit speaks with President Trump

Interactive Source: YouTube.com

Original Production Year: ***2018***

MJ News Update: That moment when preparation meets opportunity is how I can best describe this production. I stayed outside of the White House for over one hour to get a clearance. Once I was let in, it was too late to enter the room where President Trump was speaking but the Press Room was available and that was perfect for me. I didn't take my coat off because I didn't want to get too comfortable because comfort isn't what console's you in Washington. You must be ready for combat at any moment. Meeting such remarkable people is what I appreciate the most and they have gone to do some miraculous things in the world.

Turning Point USA Black Leadership Summit Revives the American Dream

The American Dream! What does that look like? Perhaps it's a non-binding powerful declaration with inspirational words to read when you're having a bad day. Moreover, many are aiming for it. But what happens when the vision of achieving the dream is more vivid for a few or sort of like *deja vu* for many?

Has the dream become a fairy tale of fear, lost in translation with many people waking up from a coma of false progress and keeping hope alive? Or, is America currently going through a modern-day rebellion of ideology? What happened to *"We hold these truths to be self-evident, that all men are created equal that they are endowed by their Creator with*

certain unalienable Rights, that among these are Life, Liberty, and the pursuit of Happiness."

What about economic stability, identity, and security of our nation? Have these foundations slipped away from the American Dream floating in cloud space not tangible for citizens to reach on land? Turning Point USA has a plan, whether a person\'s dream is cloudy, clear, distorted, or a fairy tale. They are committed to helping students reach their full potential so that their visions become a reality through leadership opportunities.

"Late to bed, early to rise, work like hell and organize," is their motto. Educating students about the importance of fiscal responsibility, free markets, and limited government is their mission. Turning Point USA believes that every young person can be enlightened to true free market values. Recently, Turning Point USA held the Young Black Leadership Summit (YBLS) in Washington, D.C. A weekend filled with special events for student leaders who are making a difference in their communities.

The YBLS attendees had the opportunity to meet the President of the United States, Donald J. Trump. Surprisingly, there are plenty of student leaders that share a similar sentiment and believe in the plan the President has put forth to *"Make America Great Again."* "Each of you *represents the future of our nation,"* President Trump told the energetic and passionate student leaders.

The young Black leaders expressed their love of the land by chanting "USA" during the

President's remarks. *"You're demanding a better kind of politics in America,"* President Trump said. Before ending his speech he informed the young Black leaders that it's okay for them to embrace free thought, and free speech, along with emphasizing using terms like beautiful and handsome are okay.

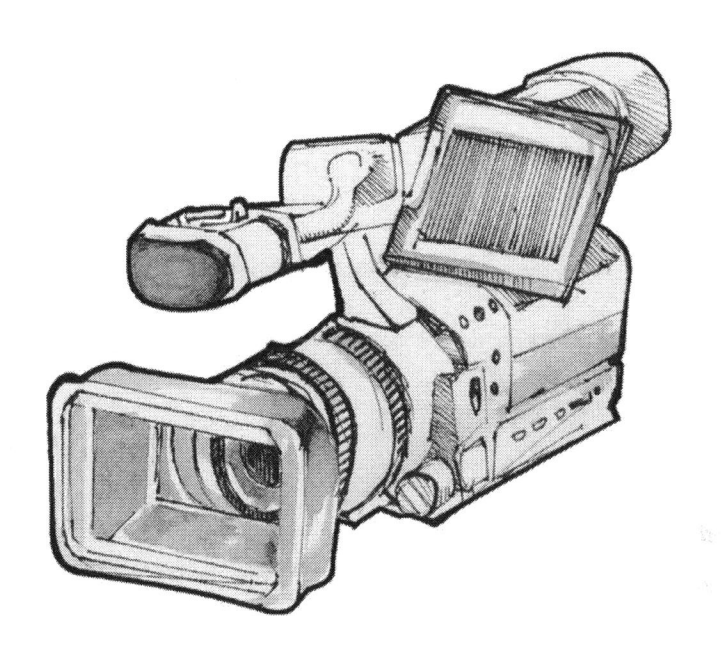

Title: Reform, rhymes and reasons for change

Interactive Source: YouTube.com

Original Production Year: ***2018***

MJ News Update: Philly rapper Meek Mill had just been released from jail and he made an appearance at the Congressional Black Caucus Annual Legislative Conference. The room was packed and many were present to hear what would be said. Politicians have a way to play on the hearts and minds of the people so this was an interesting panel discussion. I also remember how Michael Eric Dyson was very disrespectful towards the only woman on the panel and you can see it in the clip.

Reform, rhymes and reasons for change in the criminal justice system

Many celebrities have made an effort to fight for reforming the criminal justice system in

America, as it relates to harsher penalties for African Americans. Move over Kim Kardashian, the Dream Chasers are back on the scene, and Meek Mill is ready to fight to reform the criminal justice system. Platinum rap artist Meek Mill is on a mission with a plan to push for changing the terms of probation upon release from prison.

Recently, Representative Hakeem Jeffries (*NY-08*) held a forum panel discussion on "Music,

Criminal Justice and Racial Equality," featuring rap artist Meek Mill, Jeffrey Harteston, Michelle R. Scott, Dr. Michael Eric Dyson and moderated by Van Jones. The purpose of the panel is to explore the complexities, illuminate the supportive influence of modern-day musicians on activism, and discuss ways that artists can produce popular and politically engaged music.

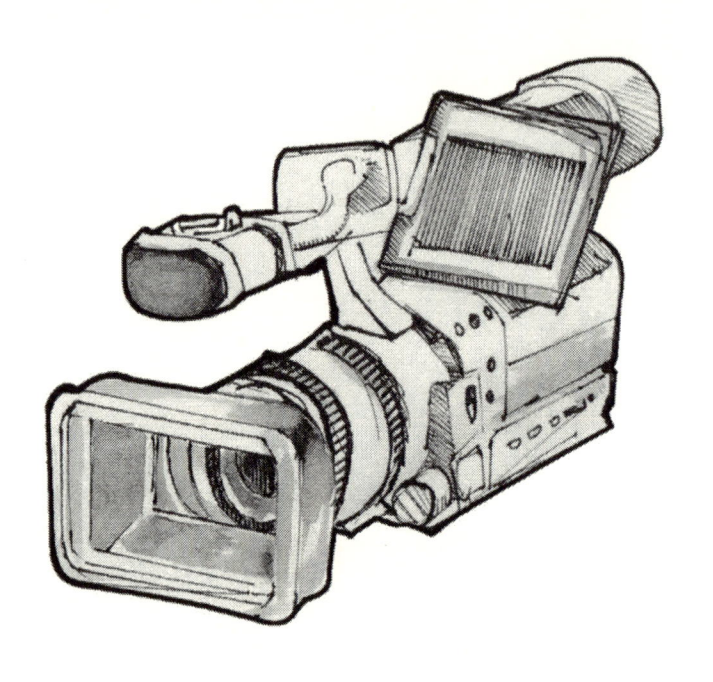

Title: Journalists share their experience in an era of Trump

Interactive Source: YouTube.com

Original Production Year: ***2018***

<u>***MJ News Update:***</u> Just because they work for a news station doesn't automatically transfer that they are a journalist. Being recognized by the court of law is the best way to distinguish yourself from the typical reporter. Being neutral in your stance is essential to your coverage. You don't want your personal feelings to come out in your piece or production. Always maintain

the ethics of journalism and that added value is how the content doesn't expire nor get outdated.

Reporting in the Era of Trump requires fair and balanced news

The days of traditional television news-station style reporting have since faded to bars and tones. Furthermore, it is transitioning into a new stream; digital news media. Much more innovative in its appeal and approach, readily accessible, along with variety, digital news content has changed the game dynamically, with a drastic impact on the industry. Without having to search further, the shift is evident from ad revenue generated by traditional news stations to currently being divided among multiple content providers for platforms such as YouTube.

Journalism in America has turned from the traditional television to a more advanced and accessible smartphone. The advancements have allowed networks to deliver news at a 3G speed or a 5G speed. However, since these industry advances, much jolting and gibberish have become the subtle standard for journalists without any regard for morals or ethical standards. What\'s fair and balanced news during the Trump Administration? I suppose it all lies in the byline. The best practices are to avoid bias, liable, defamation, slander, malicious intent, and always have credible sources; they help combat "fake news."

In the event you're short of a lead for an original beat, consider President Donald Trump's tweets for some thought on an angle. But be sure to always conduct your research. These are just some helpful tips to avoid falling into the category of "fake news," during reporting in an era of Trump. Moreover, click the video to learn about "Black Journalist Reporting: Our Experience in the Era of Trump." A panel discussion presented by Rep. Clarke for Congress featuring White House Correspondent April Ryan, and many more.

America's Most Unwanted Protest, Unite the Right

Sunday morning started out with the soothing sounds of the birds chirping. No signs of rain showers in the sky; setting the tone for the most unwanted protest in America's history, #Unitedtheright2. August 12, the day America could not make any sense out of the civil rights protest for whites, organized by Jason Kessler.

Some protestors from the Black Lives Matter NYC, made their way down the New Jersey Turnpike to come to Washington, D.C. to counter the Unite the Right protest. Another group is known as NYC Antifa also came to counter the protest rally – perhaps not to leave traces of destruction from their visit during the Inauguration. The counter-protest appeared to draw in a much larger crowd than Unite the Right rally supporters.

"My number one priority is for everyone to be safe", Jason Kessler stated. It appears that **#UnitetheRight2** had much more mainstream coverage than protest rally participants. According to Kessler, many supporters opted-out for safety reasons; not wanting Antifa to use tactics of violence for those expressing free speech.

If you search the **#Unitetheright** hashtag, anyone was able to follow America\'s most unwanted protest in modern-day history. Possibly, technology has played a role in our perception of America's history, but what exactly is a "white nationalist" or a "white supremacist" in 2018? Webster's New Pocket Dictionary defines a nationalist as an advocate of national independence. The dictionary defines a supremacist as a person advocating the supreme power or authority of a certain group.

Unite the Right organizer Jason Kessler denounced being described as a "white nationalist". He told an encircled group of reporters at the rally that he is a "civil rights advocate for white people." Demonstrating his advocacy work while millions watch, alongside his small support group, Kessler said: "a lot of people have fought and died for our Constitutional right and I won't be the one to give it up."

According to the United States trends on Twitter, it was **#UnitetheRight** versus **#ShutdownDC**. **#Unhinged** Omarosa Newman was caught in the middle of leading America's most unwanted protest aimed at preserving the civil rights of whites or countering the rights of whites. However, that's a story for a different day and a reflection of the President who does nothing to confront the AltRight.

 Luckily for **#UnitetheRight** organizer and demonstrator did exude the character of peacefully assembling for the protest of white civil rights in America in 2018. Security in the city was very secure. In fact, from clips of the protest it was an eyesore to spot Unite the Right, right in the middle of all the police protection. Mayor Bowser did mention she will use all resources to keep everyone safe, and it appeared to be the case.

The Fight for White Civil Rights?

Amid a $1.3 billion infrastructure project, Washington Metro Area Transit Authority must also contend with the **#UnitetheRightprotest** demonstration in Washington, D.C. on August 12th. Many **#UnitetheRight** supporters will gather in Virginia to demonstrate at Lafayette Park in DC.

Protest organizer and activist, Jason Kessler tweeted "my intent is to make the case for why white rights should be part of the conversations to prevent extremism. Especially as white people are facing lowered life expectancy, dwindling population, demonization of our history and culture, etc."

Perhaps the Archives is the best stop to examine the U.S. Constitution before mobilizing to protest to preserve white civil rights. Does the Constitution not grant civil rights to all citizens? It also grants citizens the right to peaceful assembly which includes whites and all the other colors under the rainbow. When did it change? Maybe when Donald Trump became President of the United States.

The DC Voice went to Deanwood Metro, ahead of the projects and protest to learn if anyone knew a protest was on its way. Along with how they feel about a private transit service for white civil rights supporters.

DC Voice: Have you heard about a *#UnitetheRight* protest coming to DC? If so, what did you learn from hearing about it? Do you plan to ride Metro during that time? Have you heard of Metro providing private rail service for the protesters? If so, how do you feel about it?

Marsella, 50: No, haven't heard about a protest. I will ride it, but I don't have any money to put on it. No, I didn't hear about Metro providing private rail service.

Marvin Hernandez: No, haven't heard about a protest. If it is don't know main goal of protest. I haven't heard of Metro providing private rail service for protesters.

Byrd: No, haven't heard about a protest. I guess I will ride Metro during a protest, I got to get to work. No, I didn't hear about Metro providing private rail service.

Michael: No, haven't heard about a protest. Yeah, I will still ride Metro during a protest. No, I didn't hear about Metro providing private rail service.

Thomas: No, haven't heard about a protest. I mainly ride the bus, but still would ride the train. Yes, I saw it on the news. It's a good idea to have, it won't affect me because I take the bus to and from work.

Despite who's heard of a protest or a private priority transit rail service for white civil rights defenders, people should plan ahead the weeks of August 11-26 and add extra time to their schedule. White Civil Rights Activist Jason Kessler has. He's taken time to tell supporters how to plan ahead of the scheduled work, starting with a "Rally Countdown Timer" on their website. The site gives instructions to protest participants:

6) REMEMBER: If you feel your rights are being violated in any way contact a team member for assistance.

7) Do not react with anger to anyone.

8) Don\'t forget American or Confederate flags, water, and bodycams.

The Metro will not allow the protest to interfere with their project. However, the jury is still out on whether they will make special arrangements for the protestors or not.

Title: The DC Voice talks with Kathy Henderson

Interactive Source: YouTube.com

Original Production Year: ***2018***

MJ News Update: I arrived at the Wilson Building on time by taking the Metro. This interview was sort of different because of where it took place and the timing but the content was very captivating. I really enjoy this interview and received a lovely letter from Mrs. Henderson that's still near and dear to my heart. I greatly appreciate those who value my time and effort.

The DC Voice Talks with Ward 5 Candidate Kathy Henderson at the Wilson Building

Moving from New York City to the Metropolitan City was a much different scene in the 80's. Certainly, the only skyscrapers buildings you'll see in the District is the Monument. Upon her arrival, Kathy Henderson not only found the scenery different, but how community concerns were addressed seemed much different as well. At the time, the District was known to Kathy as "Chocolate City" and during our talk she says "it still is chocolate city."

Despite the District's nicknames, it was the nuance of trash removal that prompted Kathy Henderson to do more. Especially after her local ANC informed her that she should get used to the conditions because that is how much the city cares. It was that turning point of trash pickup that Mrs. Henderson would find herself being considered for Chairperson of 5D ANC. From that moment Mrs. Henderson has been a champion for change when it's concerning constituents of Ward 5.

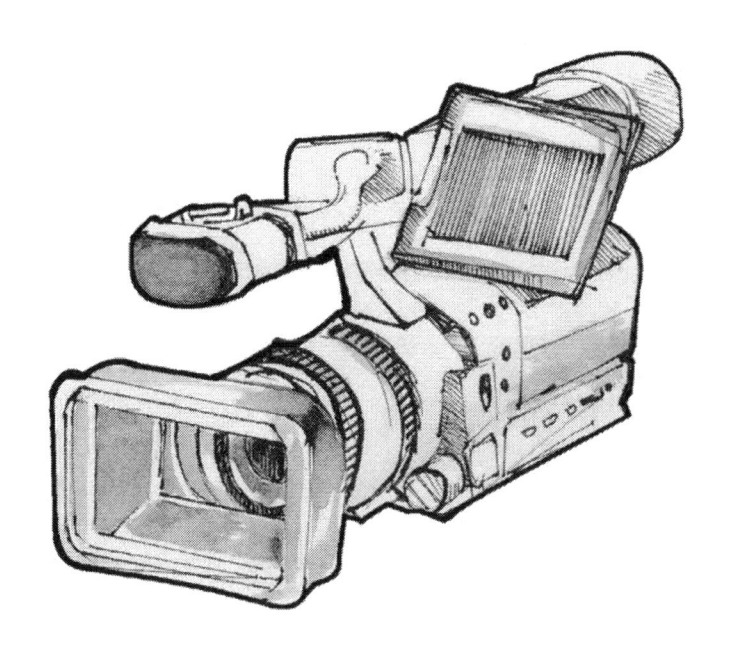

Title: Chai Tea & Chat with Gayle Hall-Carley Candidate Ward 5 Council

Interactive Source: YouTube.com

Original Production Year: ***2018***

<u>MJ News Update:</u> Implementing a new reporting style can be a hit or miss, but this was definitely a hit. I wanted to conduct this interview in a more relaxed setting and not stick to any political structure but ask the right questions. I really am proud of how the interview came out.

Chai Tea and a Chat with Gayle Hall-Carley Candidate for Ward 5 Council

Friday mornings in the District are most certainty changing! Clear skies and hot temperatures have arrived just in time for the campaign season. And starting it off with medium Chai tea to talk about the 2018 Primary Elections that are heating up, is quite refreshing! The candidates for Ward 5 Council have been on the campaign trail ready to share their plans with the constituents in the community.

The DC Voice had an opportunity to chat with a candidate for Ward 5 Gayle Hall-Carley about her action plan which has three key components Education, Safety, and Affordable Housing.

Title: Justice for ASIF Now

Interactive Source: Vimeo.com

Original Production Year: ***2018***

MJ News Update: Being in the right place at the right time does afford some opportunity especially when it comes to delivering news that people can absolutely use. And very often I would find myself in the right place to capture the stories of the people.

Justice for ASIFA Now

The weather in the district was very decent today, despite the recent downpours mixed with cold weather temperatures. In fact, it was a great day for the Alliance for Justice and Accountability to gathered in front of the Mahatma Ghandi statue on Q Street, along with many others to send a message demanding, "Justice for ASIFA."

"Stop killings Kashmir" and *"Shame India Shame"* was what the signs read, as the people chanted "we want justice." ASIFA, an 8-year-old Kashmir girl who was kidnapped and gang rape in a temple for days, and then her body was dumped in a forest according to one of the protesters signs.

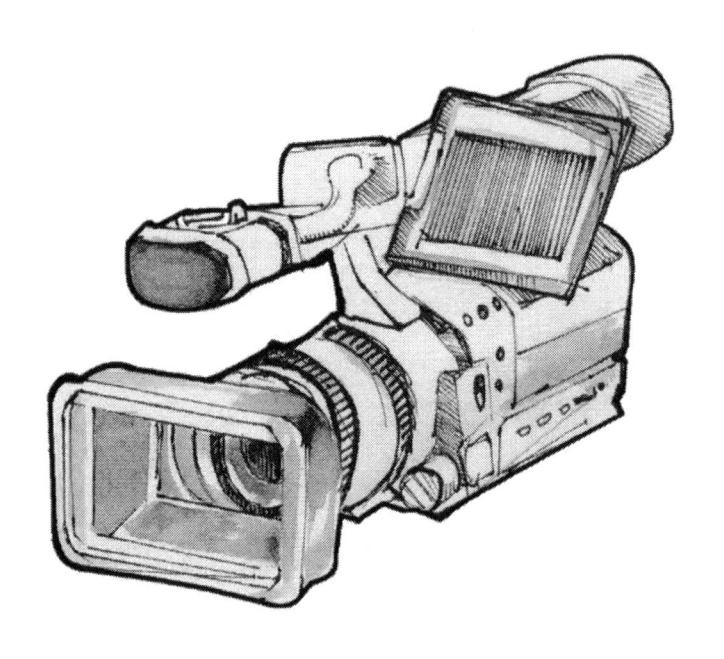

Title: The Dreamer denied, deferred, or delayed

Interactive Source: Vimeo.com

Original Production Year: ***2018***

MJ News Update: Not sure about the motives of Al Sharpton but his pattern is using a person that has deceased to build a platform off of and gain support. He is the only preacher that doesn't have a church home for all of does. DACA has since shown that it didn't work in 2024, because the Vice President Kamala Harris abandoned her border czar position and it afforded anyone and their entire family to enter the US by using a smartphone. They have since been housed in hotels and giving human capital benefits to sustain them while taxpayers are struggling. After this production I found myself being rushed to the hospital then diagnosed with walking pneumonia after my encounter with Al Sharpton.

A Dream Deferred, Denied or Caught Between DACA and Dr. King

Recently, many in America commemorated the observation of the federal holiday Martin Luther King, Jr. Day. Some contributing to service day community projects or attending ceremonies. Honoring Dr. King had a much different tone and harmony this year considering America has a new Commander-in-Chief, Donald Trump. Despite the denial of Donald Trump being President, he did honor the legacy of Dr. Martin Luther King, Jr. by signing H.R. 267 into law on January 8, "Martin Luther King, Jr. National Historic Park Act." The law re-designates a national historic site in Georgia- as the Martin Luther King, Jr. National Historical Park.

President Trump says *"The Reverend's devoting to fighting the injustice of segregation and discrimination ignited the American spirit of fraternity and reminded us of our higher purpose."* Not sure if Dr. King saw Donald Trump becoming President of the US in his dream, but much has changed from those dark days of despair in Montgomery Alabama. We still must discover a 21st century method for Voting Rights considering the Civil War ended in 1865, but we shall overcome.

During Dr. King's "Prayer Pilgrimage" to the Lincoln Memorial in Washington DC did he have a vision from God of the DREAM Act? *"I have a dream that one day this nation will rise up to live out the true meaning of its creed: We hold these truths to be self-evident, that all men are created equal."* This is only one excerpt from his dream. But it is this one phrase from his dream, which has a distorted view for many in America now. Dr. King's legacy can be linked to an instrumental civil rights movement in America\'s history. In 1956, Martin leads the Montgomery Bus Boycott, which ended in victory, when the Supreme Court ruled segregation on buses illegal. The civil rights movement challenged the Declaration of Independence through organizing marches. Demonstrating their use of civil rights which lead to over 250,000 people gathering to listen to his famous 1963 *"I Have a Dream Speech."*

Roughly, 55 years ago the conditions in America for one subgroup of the population were less than civilized and deemed illegal in most cases. Colored Americans, or the Negro as many were called, were beaten, denied the right to vote and not many education opportunities. Moreover, the living wage was far from obtaining since colored Americans and white Americans had separate water fountains, bathrooms, and couldn't even dine together. This particular ideology conflicted with the creed of the nation, therefore much change needed to take place.

Many white Americans believed that colored Americans were not recognized as civilized and decent humans. Many still considered the color American to be a slave although the slavery ended in 1865. Luckily for the creed which holds the fabric of the nation together known as the Declaration of Independence all Americans can dream again. *"We hold these truths to be self-evident that all men are created equal, that they are endowed by their Creator with certain unalienable rights, that among these are Life, Liberty and the pursuit of happiness."*

Much different from Martin Luther King's 1963 *"I Have a Dream"* speech, the *Development*

Relief and Education for Alien Minors Act was introduced in 2001 by Republican Senator Orrin Hatch from Utah. S. 1291-DREAM Act amends the illegal immigration reform and immigrant responsibility Act of 1996 to repeal the denial of an unlawful alien's eligibility for higher education benefits based on State residence unless a U.S national is similarly eligible without regard to such state residence. The Act directs the Attorney General to establish a procedure permitting an alien to apply for cancellation and adjustment without being placed in removal proceedings, provides for (1) expedited application processing without additional fees, (2) Confidentiality of application information.

DACA prohibits the removal of an alien who has not yet received a high school diploma or equivalent but has a reasonable opportunity of meeting the requirements under this Act. Permits such an alien to work. The Act also directs the Attorney General to report annually on the number, status, and disposition of applications under this Act.

Caught between the dreams, or wishful thinking for dreaming -but it is the dreamer who is faced with a fantasy or reality that they too will be able to enjoy -Life, Liberty and the pursuit of happiness here in America.

Time for Racial Exit Poll Data to Exit: Eliminating the Racial Divide in America

No mention of a hanging chad, or a candidate being left off of the ballot. It was simply the Alabama Senate race which ended in a not so fair win for one candidate. Rather, a tenacious task with Democratic runner Doug Jones and Republican runner Roy Moore up for the challenge, but the constituents of the state will determine who's best suitable for the seat. On December 12th, exit poll data revealed that it was the Black women of the state of Alabama which were responsible for electing Democratic runner Doug Jones to take up the task of Senator. Not sure if this data is causing more of a divide – when the only important statistic is which party the constituent is associated with to obtain the correct voting ballot.

Should exit poll data conceal certain information for privacy reasons when it accounts to your ethnic identity in voting?

Why is this data important? Possibly to give presidency to one particular race over the other. Nonetheless, the needs of the constituents in the state of Alabama, as a whole, amount to the same thing. Despite the people's efforts of time spent casting their vote for the candidate which they deemed most suitable for the Senate seat. Not so ready to concede is Republican runner Roy Moore. Moore has recently filed a lawsuit alleging that fraud has occurred in the recent Alabama Senate race. Are black women to blame for the recent voter fraud allegations in the race since they were primarily responsible? Why white women are associated with highly educated when voting? Are these the same issues which have plagued America's voting system since the right to vote? Does the data cause more of a divide than it should? It was just a year ago during the 2016 Presidential race, the data couldn't determine who were the primary racial benefactors of the election when voting. Moreover, black women were not even a thought other than mentions of what role Omarosa would play in the White House.

As certain segments of our population advance such as technology, education, and banking, is it time for America's voting system to advance and overhaul itself? Sort of like purge the old system. Rebuild a sound internal infrastructure which is subject to only revealing the party an American is associated with for exit poll data. How should black women feel now, knowing that they have been attached to allege voting fraud? How will this stigma affect them? Why is the black woman now being associated with dishonesty where it really plays a role – at the voting polls? Why are white women associated with education advancement in exit poll data?

Maybe "Make America Great Again" can start where it began at the exit polls. Anything is possible, but not sure if a certain segment of the population likes to be associated with voter fraud when casting a vote is not that complicated.

Is the Constitution of the United States of America Fading?

We recently celebrated Cristobal Colon, an Italian explorer who apparently discovered the *"New World,"* but many oppose his story. Being that the West was preoccupied upon his arrival; he may have been subject to reclaiming his time and taking over the terrain. Luckily, the start of the "New World" didn't begin with this questionable discovery, and our four fathers discovered their ability to form the *Declaration of Independence*.

When in the course of human events, it becomes necessary for one people to dissolve the political bands which have connected them with another, and to assume among the powers of the earth, the separate and equal station to which the Laws of Nature and of Natures God entitle them, a decent respect to the opinions of mankind requires that others should declare the causes which impel them to the separation.

We hold these truths to be self-evident, that all men are created equal, that they are endowed by their Creator with certain unalienable Rights that among these area Life, Liberty, and the pursuit of Happiness.

Oh, say can you see – if it weren't for the freeing of the states, along with the slaves, the *Constitution of the United States of America* would be confined with certain limitations for slaves. Thank God, the states and the slaves have been free at last. Now we can *"Make America Great Again."* Due to the heighten surface of racism along with racial hate groups peacefully assembling, many in America are uncertain as to the process or procedure to "Make America Great Again." Some are afraid history may repeat the most horrific time in America, slavery.

For now, President Donald Trump has been demonstrating his ability to cross over barriers and connect with all American's regardless of religion, race, or creed. It is evident by his use of social media, particularly a platform called Twitter with 140 characters. However, not all of President Trumps tweets are so sweet, as they are short; but in time the American people will determine how effective his use of technology has been during his term. From the reports of mainstream media, many American's don't find Trump's Presidential conduct a badge of honor, but it has proven to be a useful tool for him considering his communication barriers with mainstream media. Along with embellishing stories to generate more advertising revenue.

Making America Great Again can be analyzed as all sort of rhetoric, but as of late, looks like it can be applied to reclaiming the Constitution of the United States of America. Despite the Presidential election being over almost a year ago, some news outlets want to spin and wash the story until the fabric has worn out. The most disregarding fact to the spin and wash is the detergent, in this case we could consider it Tide. Former First Lady Hillary Clinton's cup of detergent was not as sustainable to help clean up some of the stains that have affected the American people. Unlike the Apprentice Presidential runner, Donald Trump\'s detergent had a smell that was more pleasant for the American people, according to the polls.

Much time is being spent on if Russia interfered in the 2016 Presidential Election. Not sure how much it's adding up to, but time will tell. The silent sentiment resides in which sector of the American people voted for the Apprentice. However, we have yet to determine or pinpoint specifically which demographic cast their vote for Donald Trump. The real news story lies in the threads of our Constitution which seems to be challenged 140 characters at a time. Some American's feel President Trump deserves a chance, and one American even considered limiting freedom of speech while on a "60 Minutes" segment.

Most recently *"Repeal the Second Amendment"* was trending on twitter. I was very shocked, and joined the thread tweeting "Really, this must apply in social media guidelines in the second paragraph." Moreover, it wasn't until after a massive shooting in Las Vegas wounding over 500 people, and killing over 50 incident citizens, that the trend had become trendy. Before this trendy twitter tag, many protests which spread throughout College and University campuses in America, weren't perceived as peaceful, such as Charolettesville, SC. US Attorney Jeff Sessions delivered a speech at Georgetown Law stating *"Freedom of thought and speech on the American campus are under attack," Sessions said during a speech to Georgetown Law School. "The American university was once the center of academic freedom — a place of robust debate, a forum for the competition of ideas. But it is transforming into ... a shelter for fragile egos."*

The 2nd Amendment to the US Constitution of the United States reads – *A well regulated Militia, being necessary to the security of a free State, the right of the people to keep and bear Arms, shall not be infringed.* Considering the majority of America\'s states are free in 2017, this right is not favorable for some since their family or friends may have been victims of gun violence. Furthermore, a loved one could have been a victim of excessive use of a firearm by a police officer, nonetheless, American's have the right to bear arms under the US Constitution.

There is ongoing discussion on Capitol Hill centered on creating common ground dialogue in classifying certain firearms and there functions. Furthermore, it is rather late considering the act of terror which took place October 1st in Las Vegas. This terrorist act was conducted by white male Stephen Paddock who was 64. Have we been relying on the same conversations and symbolism as a form of change, while our Constitutional rights are being challenged? Not sure if Colin Kaepernick's approach to hold true to his

Constitutional right lies in the symbolism of taking a knee; or creating an active policy measure which is more meaningful for the outcome of injustice and police brutality plaguing the African American communities. But considering we are at odds with North Korea, President Trump wants them "son's of bitches" off the field for taking a knee during the National Anthem at football games as he perceives it as disrespectful.

Is kneeling really a symbol of submission? Similarly to when the man proposes to a woman for marriage. Has kneeling translated into any effective outcomes of measurable policy other than loss of advertising revenue for television stations? It appears to be more of a challenge to protect our 1st Amendment right – *Congress shall make no law respecting an establishment of religion, or prohibiting the free exercise thereof; or abridging the freedom of speech, or of the press; or the right of the people peaceably to assemble, and to petition the Government for a redress of grievances.*

From kneeling to marching, what is the ultimate objective? Is it the same wash and spin cycle? This time will there be any fabric remaining to "Make America Great Again?"

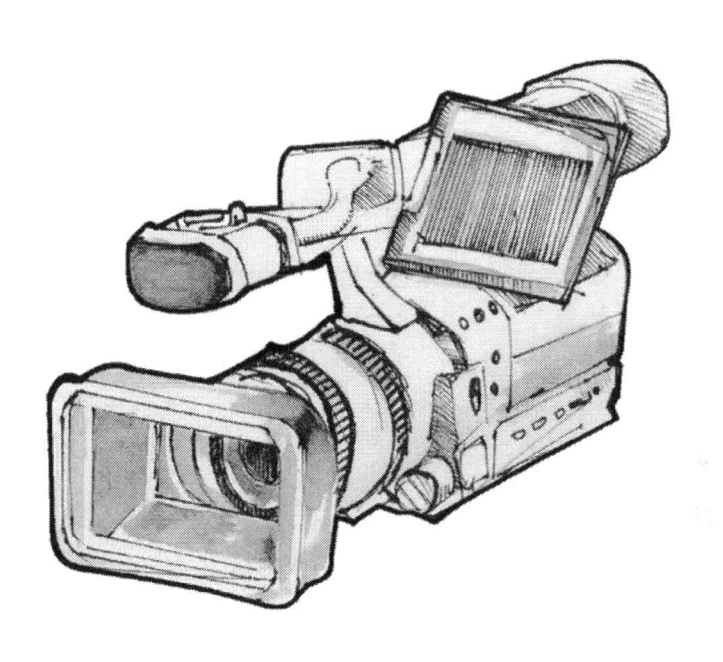

Title: Capitol Hill the People's House

Interactive Source: YouTube.com

Original Production Year: ***2021***

MJ News Update: *"This is what democracy feels like"* is the usually chant during marches sponsored by George Soros Open Society Foundation. However, the Save America Rally had an energy and feel of freedom liberty and justice for all. Millions of people watched the rally from home, but it didn't compare to being in Washington that day. Luckily, for me I left before the Capitol building was breached and I'm glad. However, my digital content was compromised causing me to re-upload the video. This was truly the last brave hearts of America. Not sure what Greek philosophy was to reduce the energy and experience to J6, but members of Congress formed an entire Committee to catch the corporate and it appears that some of them weren't so honest in their communication about what really transpired. What you see is not always what you get especially in Washington. Moreover, every journalist should have been present with boots on the ground this day because this is the start of America's history in the 21st century.

Will American Values survive a Biden Harris Election glitch Administration?

Roughly fourteen days ago thousands of Americans arrived in Washington to attend the

#SaveAmericaRally bearing witness to the Electoral College vote along with hearing President Donald Trump speech at the White House ellipse. According to President Trump's Twitter account that has since been banned- the event was going to be *"wild."* After many road closures and hotel accommodation being scaled down for those attending the rally, Stop the Steal organizer Ali Alexander suggested they would crowd source tents if need be. That was determined after Mayor Bowser had huddled with her team to secure the logistics for the rally that she informed Washingtonian's not to attend.

What a conscious effort of those people who wanted to be in Washington, attending the Save America Rally to witness an end to America as they once knew, or the beginning of something they have never experienced in modern history? The large crowd at the White House must of arrived extra early for that standing space only. While President Trump was delivering his remarks, some people decided to take a lead, marching to the Capitol ahead of the thousands that were still standing listening to the speech. The President's speech was going on simultaneously with the Electoral vote on the Chamber floor.

The Capitol grounds had been closed off to the People during the vote. According to Article II, Section 1 of the United States Constitution, *"Each State shall appoint, in such Manner as the Legislature thereof may direct, a Number of Electors, equal to the Whole Number of Senators and Representatives to which the State may be entitled in the Congress; but no Senator or Representative, or Person holding an Office of Trust of Profit under the United States, shall be appointed an Elector. The Electors shall meet in their respective States, and vote by Ballot for two Persons, of whom one at least shall not be an Inhabitant of the same*

State with themselves. The President of the Senate shall, in the Presence of the Senate and House of Representatives, open all the Certificates, and the Votes shall then be counted."

While standing behind the barricades on the Capitol grounds, some people took a citizen's position to ask permission to reach the Capitol stairs. To which the Capitol Hill police went to consult with senior leadership to learn if their request was granted or denied. Despite some of the people's willingness to obey law and order, a crowd in attendance at the rally were really anxious dismembering the barricades, ultimately inviting themselves onto the Capitol grounds. Eventually filling in what was once an empty space.

The stairs were sufficient standing ground for some of the Save America Rally supporters. It appears some in attendance on January 6th; had a different set of Rally logistics not a part of the main event. They eventually stormed the Capitol building, conducting uncivilized activities and Congressional roles. The first act was taken upon role of Speaker of the House, removing her laptop, while leaving a photo on social media to later measure the moment on a worldwide viral scale. But the scope was unprecedented, sending Congress into a lockdown.

Luckily, I left by that stormy occasion for which we still have yet to know the exact time. However, it had to occur between the hours of 2:06 pm on January 6, 2021, and, between, or after 2:37 p.m., or unknown. Again, I wasn't present to witness that Electoral College interruption. However, those are the times I had last took a photo a video. It was very interesting that this original digital content video took a few days to publish, but here's a recap! Just remember it is a strong possibility that now is a great time to screenshot the United States Constitution or remember your American value's and hold time near and dear to your heat space because they may be subject to disappear under a Biden Harris Election glitch administration. Similar to how 75 million votes just did a Dominion dance. Do you think you can dance with the agenda of a Biden Harris Administration? Here's a list of song agenda to play and possibly move you beyond a buss it challenge, or twerk on Washington, but we are awaiting the first 100 days of this unity desire driving

Administration after such display of uncivilized behavior for the last four years under a Trump Administration.

"Our allegiance is not to the special interests' corporations or global entities, it's to our children, our citizens, and to our nation itself." -President Donald Trump, 1/19/21 Farewell Address

Chapter Three TECHNOLOGY

America's Tech Giants Opt-Out of Idea of Being Regulated like Utilities

Early arrival to advanced technology hearings on Capitol Hill is suggested but not required. It's always a busy day on Capitol Hill. However, it's not until a committee hearing that most constituents get to hear their congressional representative speak beyond the pitch to get their votes. The House of Representative Judiciary Committee recently held a hearing "**Facebook, Google, Twitter: Examining the Content Filtering Practices of Social Media Giants.**" The Rayburn Building was in rare form on July 17 during the tech hearing.

A Different Demographic Line-Up

The line leading into the chambers for the hearing was rather lengthy. Consisting of many intellectual millennial; rather tech-savvy, straightforward, and ready for the proceedings.

Will filtering practices resort in being regulated like a utility or will social media giants continue to dominate the markets? It was time for the tech-savvy intellectual millennial to hear the artificial intelligence (AI) plea. They would also endure the "pardon" for the lack of urgent care and concern to protect the user\'s private information by social media giants like Facebook.

Couple that with these giants not wanting any oversight while vowing to be transparent. How dare Congress consider the idea for tech giants to be regulated like a utility! Suppose for a minute committee members might consider eating their greens to gain strength to set some guidelines for these market leaders.

Chairman Bob Goodlatte, Chair of the House Committee on the Judiciary, opened the hearing asking why tech giants should be treated differently from hotels, nightclubs, and even homeowners. "Society as a whole is finding it difficult to define what these social media platforms are and what they do," said Goodlatte during his opening remarks.

Facebook's Head of Global Policy Management, Monika Bickert informed the committee

that "Facebook is a place users have a choice and advertisers have a choice."

Furthermore, she emphasized that Section 230 of the Communications Decency Act of 1996 provides immunity from liability for providers and users of an interactive computer service.

How did America's tech giants arrive on the Hill from the Valley in the first place? It all began during the 2016 presidential election when foreign actors were able to spread political discourse using social media platforms. The result was the most bizarre outcome of a presidential election in America's history. Donald J. Trump became commander-in-chief. It was later revealed that an estimated 87 million social media user's private data had been breached. Now Congress along with America's tech giants must learn what methods of prevention these platforms plan to put forth to protect our democracy. I'm not sure these tech giants want to hear any consideration of them serving as a utility during the hearing, but something must be done.

Most recently, Facebook had another embarrassing moment during its "First Class World Premier Publishing Editorial Clearing" house phase when there was no computer recognition of one of the most important documents in America's history; The Declaration of Independence. Meanwhile, the company has yet to mention its processing method for restoring user's data that was compromised during the Cambridge Analytica data breach. However, users are expected to trust that no more third-parties will have unauthorized access to their data. These are pretty transparent data points, demanding the need for regulation to ensure oversight of user's data.

Since the hearing, Twitter has updated its interface, moved a few tabs around, and slowed down its connection, it appears. Unless that is the service provider not up to speed on the spectrum, but that's a different story. I'm not sure what the tone of the next hearing will be, but be sure America's tech giants don't want to hear the word "*utility.*"

MJ News Update: In 2024, the Department of Justice is considering behavioral and structural remedies that would prevent Google from using products such as Chrome, Play, and Android to advantage Google search and Google search-related products and features. The Department of Justice is also suggesting to limit or prohibit default agreements and "other revenue-sharing arrangements related to search and search-related products.

Understanding License, Terms, and Use of Technology

Has anyone ever considered looking up at the clouds and thinking "only if I knew what cloud space is?" or "what could possibly be considered the Internet of Things?" Perhaps the first measure to acceptance is understanding. Let's take it a spectrum further. What if consumers understood the *"Internet of Things"* and the role it plays while operating their smart devices?

Maybe if more people understood *what* and *how* the internet works that would ease much uncertainty among consumers and stakeholders alike. Many stakeholders look at security first when considering the *"Internet of Things."* Suppose it is first beneficial to them, but it is the consumer who gets the best utilization from the tools and services. Besides, how does the company know what to secure if it doesn't understand its network operating system, needless to mention how to comply with regulations.

When consumers purchase a computer, smartphone, or smartwatch they must first read instructions on how to operate the device. Once they have gain some understanding of the device's use, then they must secure their systems. Some consumers tend to opt-out of reading the instructions and going straight to application download mode, without any sense of security. Often consumers are unaware of the third-party access behind the applications. And most likely who they give access to, plays a major role. Suppose the consumer or company doesn't update their security access systems for nearly four years, then a security breach is most likely to occur.

Last month, Facebook's CEO Mark Zuckerberg had to testify before Congress during a hearing to determine how a foreign company was able to steal private information from millions of platform users. Mark suggested one of the objectives to the plan was restricting the amount of access and information developers will have going forward. However, Mr. Zuckerberg said,*"security is never a solved problem."* Facebook also plans to conduct a full audit of the foreign companies' information systems and if that doesn't work they intend to take legal action. During the Facebook hearing US

Senator Lindsey Graham (R-SC) stated *"most Americans have no idea what they are signing up for because Facebook terms of service are beyond comprehension."* A few hours later during the hearing Senator Jon Tester (D-MT) suggested that Facebook license is *"very thick."*

While technology advances daily, are the policies and regulations on the same spectrum as the functions and use of the internet – attempting to connect and link a definition to the terms, use, and license of *"Internet of Things?"* Lately, we have learned that the internet is a tool of many features, but most importantly being able to understand the meaning to apply any effective measure has yet to be a milestone marked at the moment. A functional definition could be a universal starting point for both the stakeholder and the consumer. Perhaps that's very complex, similar to the *"Internet of Things."*

Today's *"Emerging Tech DC"* panel discussion powered by Public Knowledge ask that milestone marker question, *"What is the Internet of Things?"* The most honest reply from a male developer on the panel was *"I don't know."* It is better to be safe than sorry in this constantly changing technology space – so stating when you don't know is rather preferred and tech forward thinking. The IoT presents an opportunity to improve and enhance nearly every aspect of our society, economy, and day-to-day lives suggested during a *"Cyber security of the Internet of Things"* hearing by the subcommittee. Representative Will Hurd, Chairman of the subcommittee stated that in order for us to be able to fully harness this technology, the Internet of Things needs to be built with security in mind and not as an afterthought. He also suggests that when integrating these devices into our lives people need to know that they are secure.

The US Chamber of Commerce gives the description of IOT referring to networks of objects that communicate with other objects and with computers through the internet. To elaborate on that description, I took into consideration a CompTIA course at UDC Community College as another resource. During an *"NTIA Internet of Things Request for Comments,"* CompTIA provided the definitions that IoT should be used as an ecosystem of connected devices that enables the unsiloing and smartification of communication. IoT drives the potential for efficient economies and citizens facing services. This includes motion sensors, vehicles, appliances, medical devices, infrastructure, and agricultural systems. With all these extra amenities added to a smart device, does this help ease the understanding of the license, terms, and use of the Internet of Things?

The Damage is Irreversible – Closed Captioning

What started as a routine location shoot to cover the Grand Opening of the MGM at National Harbor has turned into a two-year nightmare against one of America's top technology leaders. The fact that I might be subjected to deleting my body of works because of a strategic assassination of my character is deplorable. Out of 250 videos, this one has caused me the most harm. Now, I must start the removal process of all original compelling electronic media from the tech company's platform, and no longer use the services or products because of an alleged defamatory action. The nature of defamation – closed captioning.

Let's start by defining defamation. According to Bill 11-0231, *"Uniform Correction or Clarification of Defamation Act of 1995,"* introduced by Councilmember Lightfoot, defamatory means tending to harm reputation caused by the false context of a publication that is published. Economic loss caused by a false and defamatory publication. This Act also applies to all publications, including writing, broadcasts, oral, communications, electronic-transmission or other form of transmitting information. According to the law, a person may maintain an action for defamation if: 1) the person has made a timely and adequate request for correction or clarification from the defendant, or 2) the defendant has made a correction or clarification.

In 2012, it was reported by cnet that a 2- year class action lawsuit filed by the National Deaf Association in 2010 alleging the streaming service Netflix was *"failing to provide adequate closed captioning on 'Watch Instantly' streaming video programming, and therefore was in violation of the Americans with Disabilities Act."* What derived from the class action lawsuit was a decree. The decree is a model for the streaming entertainment industry. *"We are pleased to have reached this agreement and hope it serves as a benchmark for other providers of streaming video entertainment,"* according to Netflix Chief Product Officer Neil Hunt in a statement. Wonder how they went about assessing the damage done in their situation? It had to satisfy the elements of proving harm was done and being reasonable in the decision to move on for the rest of your life from the harm and hold your head high as if nothing ever happened.

Damages in the MGM situation can be assessed from two aspects. One is the aspect of defective software, and the second is the rate a glitch is most likely to occur on the tech company's platform. I believe a damage assessment classification of severe irreversible damage has been done since it cannot be fixed. The tech company's argument is *"why didn't I take it down?"* The tech company operates the largest search engine in North America, *'taking it down'* doesn't erase it from public record. I will always have an issue with accurate results, whether the system is updated or not. Once information, aka "data" is stored in a database it does not change its content or the context data file storage classification. The update is more for operational functionality.

As a result of the tech company's actions, I will be recognized in their database as a disgusting, degrading, destructive, and defamatory statement since the initial act was carried out through electronic media data file transfer. The system database has recognized and classified my identity as disgusting, degrading, destructive, and inhumane;

not civil, or credible, worthless. Words carry meaning, and have a lasting effect, do not let your words destroy or harm.

As a journalist; word choice, use, and meaning must be carefully examined because one word can change the entire context of the meaning of what I'm attempting to convey to my readers. This is where I'm most thankful for the editors of the publication to verify that the word choice flows with the context of the paragraphs. Perhaps words are great to inspire, provoke thought, and hopefully move someone to act on the words to bring them to life, similar to an action verb.

I use many words that describe the actions which are taking place at a specific time and location to bring my audience closer to the event. When that selection of words and phrases is not properly represented and contributes the misrepresentation of facts, it not only damages my credibility as a journalist, it deprives my audience interpretation and presentation of the venue I have worked so hard to bring to them. *"The damage is irreversible."*

Google CEO Doesn't Know How His Company Operates – Needs Government Guidance

It was a grandiose occasion at the Rayburn Building to welcome the biggest data collectors in America's history to share some insightful information on consumer data use. Not sure if Sundar Pichai, Google's CEO arrived by autonomous driving vehicle or plane, but the House of Representatives Judiciary Committee was ready to hear what Google has been doing with consumers\' data. This was the moment many had been awaiting since the 2016 Presidential Election. In fact, it's been so much time; an alleged Chinese search engine was under way, the secrecy of Google+ breach, YouTube service interruptions and content rankings, along with algorithms, no restrictions on child pornography, and the robots Ad purchasing power ability. As you can see it\'s a long list of items in which the hearing could possibly address a few. Therefore, it primarily focused on *"Transparency & Accountability: Examining Google and its Data Collection Use and Filtering Practices."*

Despite Pichai joining Google 15 years ago, it appears from the December 11th hearing he is disconnected from his company's day-to-day operations, standards and practices. This leaves many to question whether Google is more of a "baby" start-up company or the largest private company with access to all the worlds data with minimal security or privacy regulations. Google is not the government and needs guidance from them. The questions ranged from:

- "Who at Google makes judgment calls on whether to filter or block objectionable content?" – Committee Chairman Bob Goodlatte (R-Va), opening remarks
- "Mr Pichai is it true, the Android operating systems sends Google information every 3 minutes detailing the exact location of a smart phone?" – Committee member
- How advertising is handled at Google

- "What legal obligations is the company under to disclose such data exposure that doesn't involve financial information, [but] still involve other personal information?"

Mr. Pichai reviewed his notes but didn't have a good answer for the first question. *"We go to great lengths to protect the privacy. Android is a powerful platform, and it depends on the applications users choose to use,"* replied Mr. Pichai to smart phone data collection. It was very timely to learn that advertising rates can vary. However no bias is associated with the advertisers as many get ready for the 2020 Elections. Mr. Pichai says *"it is done in a non-partisan way."* *"It depends on the situation and all requirements,"* replied Mr. Pichai to the legal obligations to disclose data exposure.

The company shares and collaborates a lot with law enforcement. Moreover, Google CEO said during the hearing *"we do not sell users' data as a company,"* and they *"always think there is more to do."* As the company grows more mature in operating standards, privacy practices, and tracking users every move, it is likely that Google could take into consideration Congressman Steve Cohen's question: "Have you considered having an online school that people could go to, login and ask questions? Something easy to talk to somebody and ask how do I do this or that?" Google is constantly looking for better ways, and one option is online tutorials and is happy to present feedback to the Committee on this lesson plan.

During the hearing, Pichai didn't appear to know the answers to the questions and additional notes were needed. When asked an entry level question, "Are you familiar with the General Data Protection Regulations by the European Union?\" Mr. Pichai stated, *"I am very familiar."* He acknowledged that the United States does not have a comprehensive legislation. Congressman Ted Poe (R-Tx) followed up that preschool graduate question with , "Are you familiar with House Resolution 1039?" Mr. Pichai further displayed his lack of knowledge by not knowing that HR 1039 was introduced by the Congressman that would adopt some of the European practices in American and give consumers the right to privacy. A copy of which will be provided to him courtesy of the Congressman.

Google certainly has a few more weeks before the New Year to focus on growth and development regarding its operating standards. That will be coupled with the security and privacy of users' data before a formula from the government arrives. Hopefully, at the next hearing Mr. Pichai will be able to speak into the mic and answer more questions from the Committee!

Getting to Understand Privacy from a Consumers Perspective

Is there a reasonable way to adjusting your privacy settings in your smart phone? Sort of similar to the automatically unreasonable censorship standards on social media lately? Suppose Senator Jon Tester (D-MT) wouldn't have been subject to giving a scenario for

America's Tech Giants to explain during the *"Examining Safeguards for Consumer Data Privacy,"* hearing. The scenario was a regular guy, a farmer, using the internet to browse then an advertisement for tires pops up. Oftentimes that search is done through Google. *"How do they get that information?"* asked Senator Tester. To which Google replied *"we understand the complexities of the ecosystem."*

What do consumers really understand about their privacy to even consider operating a function in their smartphone privacy settings? I recently conducted a survey to learn **"How Much Consumers Understand About Privacy."**

Prior to the survey results, America's Tech Giants gave a reasonable meaning, along with qualified responses of privacy. Their testimonies were before the Senate Committee on Commerce, Science, and Transportation during the *"Examining Safeguards for Consumer Data Privacy"* hearing.

According to Apple's submitted testimony to the Senate, *privacy* means a fundamental human right, much more than having the right to not share your personal information. Users can decide whether to share personal information and with whom. Privacy is about living in a world where you can trust that your decisions about how your personal information is shared, used, and respected. During the same time, Twitter submitted their testimony which read they must be a trusted, and healthy place in order for freely exchange of ideas and information to continue. Their testimony also read that privacy is part of Twitter\'s DNA. Luckily, Senator Warren didn't have to contribute her recent DNA results to their testimony.

Twitter suggest they offer a range of ways for people to control their experience on the platform. That deliberate design has allowed people using Twitter to protect their privacy.

Now let's learn the results of the survey conducted *October 6, 2018* near the Washington Monument. The survey is comprised of the following questions: *What do you consider as your privacy? Do you know how to adjust your privacy settings to opt-out of third-party Ads?*
Would you give a third-party your privacy information? The final question on the survey, *what does privacy mean to you?*

- "It's like an atomic bomb Bob Marley says doesn't stop time."
- "Safety and security,"
- "means a lot,"
- It's like a bubble, pop it when doing something I don't like."
- "important"
- "securing is important"
- "having a personal life, and not public"
- "safeguarding personal and private transactions"

Who Will Shape Consumer Privacy Laws Using Common Sense Standards?

The 21st century can be classified as the *"Technology Industrial Revolution Era,"* with **data** being the market's driving force. Companies leading the driving force must now generate a starting point from which to shape laws designed to protecting consumer's privacy.

The Dirksen Senate Office Building was where the hearing *"Examining Safeguards for Consumer Data Privacy,"* originated. The meeting was led by U.S. Senator John Thune, Chairman of the Senate Committee on Commerce, Science, and Transportation. *"This hearing will provide leading technology companies and Internet service providers an opportunity to explain their approaches to privacy, how they plan to address new requirements from the European Union and California, and what Congress can do to promote clear privacy expectation without hurting innovation,"* says Chairman Thune.

This era has amassed $1 Trillion dollars in revenue despite not having a framework or formula for protecting consumer privacy.

Everyone contributes to the Technology Industrial Revolution whether demanding accessibility to websites and applications or supplying the products and services. Shaping the laws must include both aspects; creativity and innovation. This era has amassed $1 Trillion dollars in revenue despite not having a framework or formula for protecting consumer privacy. Consumer data increasingly floats in the cloud and the Internet of things (IOT) with limited protections for consumers. The only safeguard at this point is navigating to find a way to opt-out. The IOT also allows for more transmission of private information that needs to be secured and stored.

Since this wasn't a "gotcha hearing," companies leading the Technology Industrial Revolution Era such as Amazon, Apple, AT&T, Google, and Twitter had an opportunity to give their testimonies addressing ways they currently protect consumer's privacy. Their message included a willingness to sketch out a solution with the exact limits and conditions for securing consumer's privacy beyond the current navigating to opt-out.

There should also be guidelines for protecting consumer privacy, advertisers, creation and innovation

Whether or not the companies are sketching a shape that would be well rounded, confusion can arise as to who controls consumer's privacy and how to access those controls. This potentially raises a conflict between the data owner, the consumer, and third parties wanting the data. There should also be guidelines for protecting consumer privacy, advertisers, creation and innovation, and allowing the consumer to control and access privacy preferences more easily. Sharing information should be at the consumer's discretion.

The European Union has shaped a standard the General Data Protection Regulation (GDPR) for companies to comply with. The regulation lays down rules relating to:

- the protection of natural persons with regard to processing of personal data
- the free movement of personal data, and
- protecting fundamental rights and freedoms of natural personal and in particular their right to the protection of personal data

This regulation applies to the processing of personal data wholly or partly by automated means. In accordance with the EU standard **personal data** is defined as information "relating to an identified or identifiable natural person in reference to an identifier such as name, an identification number, location data, and online identifier or to one or more factors specific to the physical, physiologic, genetic, mental, economic, cultural or social identity of that natural person."

Those regulations are rather straightforward and have been set since May of this year for compliance. Considering those regulations haven't been well received in the US, California lawmakers composed a bill **SB822** *"California Internet Consumer Protection & Net Neutrality Act of 2018,"* co-written by Democratic Senator Scott Wiener. The purpose of the bill seeks to enact various net neutrality provisions adopted from FCC regulations that were repealed in 2017. *"Internet Openness,"* is another name for net neutrality, a concept that the Internet highway should be open and equally available to all, and that no internet "traffic" should be given preference or prioritized over other traffic. SB822 would make it unlawful for internet service providers (ISP) to engage in the following:

- blocking lawful content, applications, services, or non-harmful devices, subject to reasonable network management practices
- impairing or degrading lawful internet traffic on the basis of internet content, application, or service, or use of a non-harmful device
- engaging in paid prioritization
- unreasonably interfering with or unreasonably disadvantaging either an end user's ability to select

However, that bill didn't fully protects a consumer's private information. For this reason, Senators, Troy Singleton and Joseph F. Vitale introduced **S2834.** The bill requires commercial Internet websites and online services to notify customers of collection and disclosure of personal identifiable information and allows customers to opt out. The bill requires that an operator who collects the personally identifiable information of a customer to clearly and conspicuously post on its Internet website or online service home page a link entitled "**Do Not Sell My Personal Information**". This link enables a customer to opt out of the disclosure of their personally identifiable information.

Understanding privacy laws is a serious matter for all consumers.

These bills along with regulations should be of some assistance to these leading technology companies in shaping laws to safeguard consumer privacy. Understanding privacy laws is a serious matter for all consumers. Most recently, a month before the midterm elections, Facebook announced another data breach affecting an estimated 50 million users. Twitter has found many bugs ready to corrupt their platform, and Google+ cannot control program glitches- so getting rid of the services all together is their solution.

With all these latest mishaps of data management and security, it leaves room for many questions, and exactly what constitutes as trust regarding the security of consumer privacy. Hopefully, these companies will be more accountable with data management, along with **privacy laws protecting consumer data** so Congress can give a "qualified yes" or "qualified no" to their standards of safeguarding consumer's privacy.

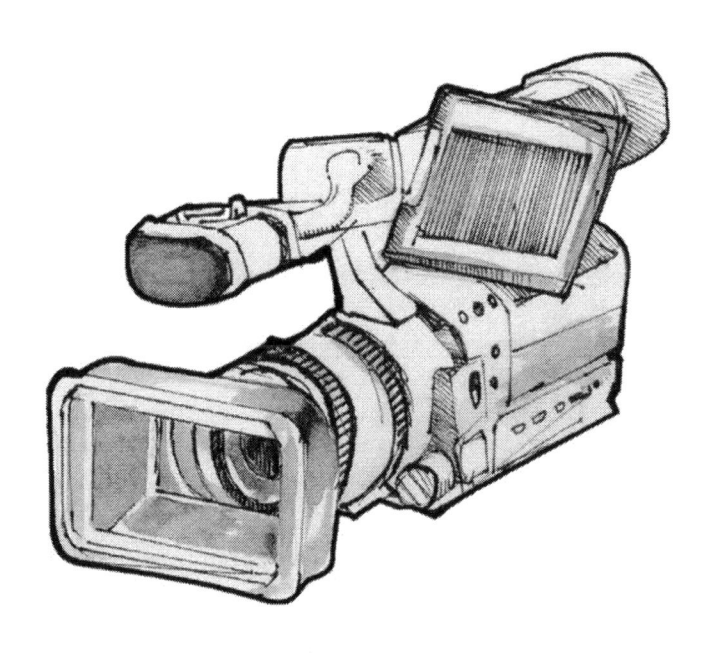

Title: TECH 2020 bridging the divide in the Valley

Interactive Source: YouTube.com

Original Production Year: ***2019***

<u>MJ News Update:</u> Everyone doesn't have the same grasp on technology as a member of the geek squad. Technology can be very tricky, glitch, and not function accordingly at times. The dependency level on technology is rather scary because it's sort of like how did one function prior to the operating system software being sold in bundle deals. The main purpose of technology is to provide a seamless functionality with minimal difficulty. Technology is often upgraded every three months so not sure it's dependable as we rely on its capabilities. Technology is only as good as the program is designed for.

TECH 2020 Helps Bridge the Divide Bringing Diversity to the Industry

What's the one word which is always talked about in some aspect every day, and people can't get enough? It also requires multiple updates, and apps to function? Technology. That's right! Not too bad, except when the device battery you're operating loses charge. Technology is changing the world around us and our dependency has shaped our reality; shifting its dynamic use. What is **technology**? A science used to solve practical problems, according to Webster's New Pocket Dictionary. Currently, technology is facing a challenge in solving practical problems by providing opportunity and employment for more minorities.

In May 2015, Congressman G.K. Butterfield along with Congresswoman Barbara Lee wanted to bridge the divide and lack of diversity in Silicon Valley, so they sparked the conversation. The conversations were centered on the focus of increasing transparency, adding African Americans to the Board of Trustees, along with more employment opportunity in government affairs offices. From those conversations came TECH 2020, a one-on-one experience engaging technology enthusiast with industry professionals that are bridging the diversity divide in the tech industry.

Hopefully, TECH 2020 is the code that creates opportunity, unity, and bridges the divide in the tech industry.

The Damage is Irreversible – If it acts like a publisher...

In my previous post "The Damage is Irreversible – Closed Captioning" I relay the position I found myself in after my post on The MGM Grand Opening. The other part of that story has to do with the communication with the tech company in trying to resolve the issue. The tech company believes sending a tweet, or tagging them in an Instagram media post is not reasonable. I'm not sure if a clause exists in their terms of service agreement that states Twitter and Instagram are not reasonable forms of communication. It would have helped if I had read the agreement from the very start but it\'s ironic that they would devalue the communicative value of their products.

There's a saying that if it walks like a duck and quacks like a duck – it's a duck. Let's consider how this analogy pertains to these social media platforms. I suppose these social media platforms are only deemed reasonable when unbiased Ads are rolling up and down the feeds. I also wonder if going to ask the FCC would be considered as reasonable, along with Congress, perhaps it depends on the person you ask. If you ask the tech company the reasonable question "if they are a news publication?," they would deny that and simply refer to being classified as a products and services company holding all the world\'s data.

During the holiday season, search results using the tech company's services could yield the best price points for your pockets; along with ranking the season's splendid items. Depending on if its election time, the products and services have news publication appeal, although they have made it clear they're not a news agency. They just store all the news information and content on platforms, products, and services in the event they go public and announce turning into a news agency. There's no need to question any biased behavior or practices, and since satisfying some news gathering elements; they could be considered a full-service news agency with their in-house news fact-checkers, and political Ad rate busters. What they don't have is a decree similar to Netflix and the National Deaf Association.

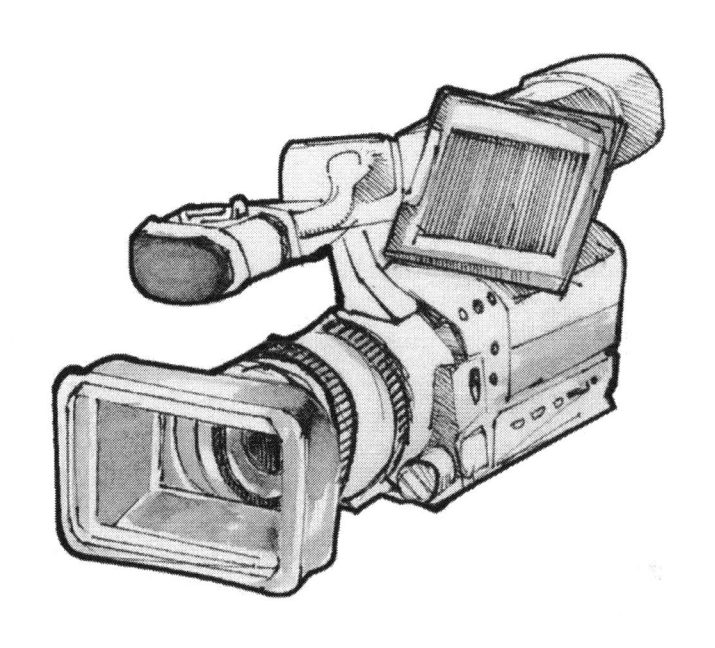

Title: Automated Vehicle Summit, Variety & Innovation

Interactive Source: Vimeo.com

Original Production Year: ***2018***

MJ News Update: The idea that a motor vehicle can drive itself is fascinating. It's far much different from setting the cruise control module on the car. A self-driving car has to really have the best technology for various reasons and especially because its operating machinery on its own and will be responsible for getting one from point A to point B. However, the idea of maintenance hasn't really been studied and from experience having a hybrid vehicle, the battery can cost

$10,000 or greater. Automated vehicles are amazing as long as it's programmed for many adventures. The gas mileage can also get greater with design.

US Department of Transportation Listens to the Public's Point of View on Automated Vehicles

What do you call a machine which requires a physical person to operate? Furthermore, it can take people or commodities from one destination to the next. Transportation, that's correct. Transportation plays a vital role in our daily lives. It allows people and parcel to arrive at a different destination using a specific mode. No matter if it is to work, school, another country, or even the supermarket, it usually requires the use of transportation. The modes of transportation vary from trucks, cars, airplanes, trains, buses, and drones. Then there are plenty of categories along with specific brands for transportation, sort of like a red '85 Chevy Impala with white interior. The key to transportation is starting the engine, moving gears in motion to arrive at a different destination the safest. Time is also a factor in transportation, not sure if construction work occupies most of the time in traffic. Efficiency plays a role also because time matters to everyone.

What important role will technology play in transportation? Given consideration to Garmin, Waze, or traditional OnStar, people who travel by mode of a car usually use a GPS device. So long to the Atlas Road maps. The GPS device helps the driver arrive at their destination of choice. The GPS gives the driver turn-by-turn directions until a phone call comes through. Technology has advanced transportation to the point where a driver can receive a telephone call in the car.

Those are just minute milestones compared to what\'s in the making. Currently, do you trust your car? Is it reliable? Does it need any repairs? What if you could sit in your car, then tell the computer operating system your destination and not have to do anything? Well, that looks to be the arrival point for some automobiles now. So long to cruise control on your road trip. The car will drive the driver. Would that then make the driver a passenger? That is sort of pushing the ignition a bit. However, policymakers have to decide.

Recently, the US Department of Transportation held a *"Public Listening Summit on Automated Vehicle Policy,"* in Washington, DC at the headquarters office building. Many were in attendance. Elaine Chao, Secretary for Transportation was the keynote speaker. The summit also had panel discussion from industry professionals. The public certainly wanted their point of view heard, and many were in attendance listening to the future of transportation take a new direction and mode.

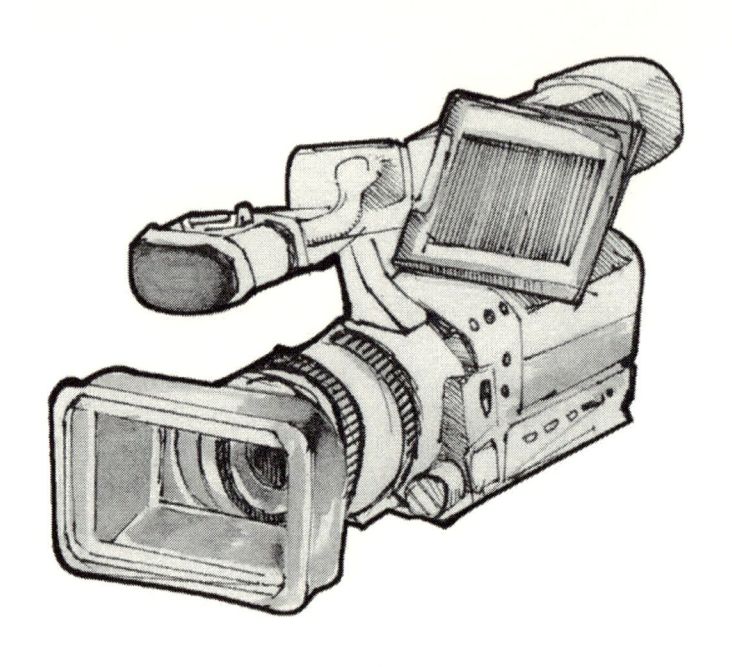

Title: Oh, Internet who shall forsake thee

Interactive Source: YouTube.com

Original Production Year: ***2017***

***MJ News Update*:** Many people have experience some form of latency or lag in the uploading process for a video. What is the cause of such slow down you might ask? It has to do with net neutrality, but the internet service provider will blame it on towers in your geographical location. It makes you really question are you getting the high-speed data connections that you pay for. As for me, I'm still working on calculating cloud storage data and have yet to get the equation right.

The FCC Ends the Year with a Rollback
Bonus: Ask your ISP for Details this Christmas

Ho! Ho! Ho! And away net neutrality goes after years of bundle deals, along with an open and free internet for consumers. What a way to make the Christmas season brighter? Sure Santa will consider the FCC and FTC on his nice behavior list while broadband companies and advertisers remain on his naughty list. Not sure how bright rolling back to Title I classification status of restoring the internet is, but we will soon find out. But don't look down aisle 5 at Walmart for the deal.

On Thursday morning, the police cars aligned the streets leading to the FCC before Santa could ever land his sleigh near. Many people stood in the frigid cold temperature protesting the actions of restoring the jurisdiction of the

Federal Trade Commission to act when broadband providers engage in anticompetitive, unfair, or deceptive acts or practices. A large portion of the American population does not have access to the internet not to mention the internet of things- while many believe their freedom to browse or surf the internet at their leisure will end. *"The FCC is not killing the internet,"* Commissioner Carr said during the Open Meeting. Thursday's vote was to restore the longstanding, bipartisan light-touch regulatory framework that has fostered rapid Internet growth, openness, and freedom for nearly 20 years.

The rollback to Title I adopted by the Commission will protect consumers at far less cost to investment than the prior rigid and wide-ranging utility rules. This framework will increase transparency to protect consumers, spur investment, innovation, and competition. Will it stop consumers from having to purchase Microsoft Office separately when in need of a new computer? It sure will be a savings for the consumer.

FTC acting Chair Maureen K. Ohlhausen issued a statement regarding the FCC stance stating *"The FCC's action today restored the FTC's ability to protect consumers and competition throughout the internet ecosystem. The FTC is ready to resume its role as the cop on the broadband beat, where it has vigorously protected the privacy and security of consume data and challenged broadband providers who failed to live up to their promises to consumers."* Furthermore, Commission Clyburn expressed during the meeting *"reclassification of broadband would do more than wreak havoc over net neutrality, it will also undermine our universal construct for years to come."* Before ending her eulogy, Commissioner Clyburn stated her sentiment for the FTC, it is an agency with know, no, none not, technical expertise and telecommunications. The FTC is an agency that may or may not even have authority over broadband providers in the first instance.

What happens next for net neutrality? Well, it will be best to locate your browser while you still have a connection search for Twitter and follow Commissioner Clyburn (@MClyburnFCC) to find out, because she plans to host a Town Hall on Twitter next Tuesday at 2 p.m. EST. Maybe viewers will learn more about internet ownership, who really has control over what consumers have access to when it is a paid service. Many sure don't have control over how to count cloud space nor if the broadband speed is really running at that rate. Just maybe these Internet Service Providers can come to a common ground that consumers just want to save more of their cash this Christmas.

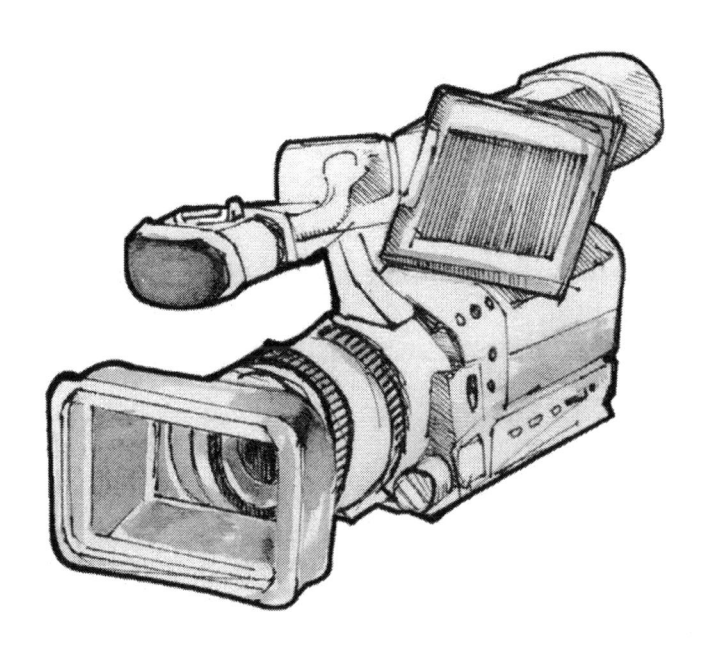

Title: The MJ Experience Tour Gallaudet

Interactive Source: Vimeo.com

Original Production Year: ***2017***

MJ News Update: The art of communication is phenomenal. And our ability to infuse technology in delivery of a message is very incredible, but we must learn why some techniques for communication are required and closed captioning is one. Closed-captioning serves one purpose and that's to ensure those who are deaf or hard of hearing can access information.

The MJ Experience: Enjoy Life and Learn, Tour Gallaudet University Museum

There's a possibility if you live in Washington, DC, or visited, you've traveled down a street called Florida Avenue. In the Northeast quadrant of the city, located in Ward 5 lies 99 acres of rich history and culture, Gallaudet University – where you can also visit the *Gallaudet Museum.*

Today's experience we explore the rich history and culture of Gallaudet University Museum with manager and curator Meredith Perruzi. Mrs. Perruzi is a graduate of Gallaudet University class of 2011.

The Gallaudet Museum promotes and interprets the rich and complex deaf experience. On your visit at the museum, you can learn about the rich history of the university which dates back 150 years. See inspiring exhibit artifacts and gain an understanding of deaf life from cultural, linguistics, and sensory perspectives.

What did I learn from this experience?

I learned that every city has its own uniqueness, but it's the people which really make the city come alive and flourish. While at the Gallaudet Museum I learned that deaf people live a life like me, and the ability to communicate across barriers requires paying attention to the person trying to deliver the message. This was a miraculous experience.

What did you think about the MJ Experience? Please comment *(The MJ Experience gives the audience an opportunity to enjoy life\'s simple pleasures, while learning as Mindy Jo explores treasures in the Metropolitan city, Washington, D.C.)*

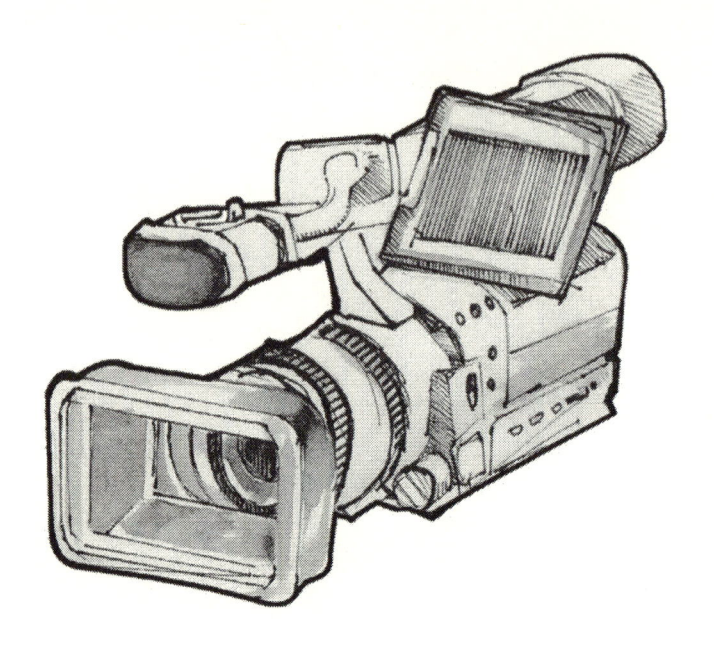

Title: Congress teach TECH a lesson

Interactive Source: Vimeo.com

Original Production Year: ***2017***

<u>***MJ News Update:***</u> What types of technology does Congress use? Currently, many members use Twitter, Facebook, and Instagram to update their constituents on what's happening and to share bills that are introduced. Moreover, those are more social construct platforms so outside of those apparatuses what type of technology do they use? Do they use customer relations management software to manage constituent data or what?

Technology only functions as good as the person who programmed the software.

Did Artificial Intelligence Ruin the 2016 Presidential Race?

Roughly twelve months ago- the people were faced with making a genuine decision; selection of who will be the 2016 President of the United States of America. Since that day American's cast their vote, many have been perplexed as to how this paramount Presidential shift occurred? Despite the debacle debates, much racial tension, taunting, slurs, and even physical attacks, the American people voted and favored Donald Trump, former reality television host and business mogul for the position over former First Lady Hillary Clinton. A year later, many are led to believe that Donald Trump had some extraterrestrial boost to help him secure the win which has resulted in a social media hearing about Russia's infamous role in the 2016 Presidential election.

Presidential Poise

Despite Donald Trump's political experience and etiquette, many people overlooked that when they cast their vote, and voted on the promise that he will *"Make America Great Again."* Although the Trump campaign took a few pointers from the Obama campaign, it was Trump's use of social media preferably the platform Twitter – that helped him get his promise out to the American people. Some are stunned as to his social media strategy. Reports have since surfaced speculating that Russia influenced the 2016 Presidential election and may have assisted his campaign as early as April 2016 to inform him that they were in possession of dirt on Hillary Clinton in the form of thousands of stolen emails.

George Papadopolous, Trump Campaign foreign policy advisor plead guilty recently. Alluding that the Russians approached the Trump campaign involving thousands of stolen emails. It is unclear if those emails detailed any information regarding Hillary Clinton and her role as Secretary of the State Department. Records indicate she responded to the request which revealed that her State Department email account had no correspondence. Clinton was formally asked to turn over her emails from her private server with 50,000 pages of emails.

From stolen emails, to rise and spread of fake news, it's been a constant battle to untangle the threads and pinpoint exactly how the Russians mounted what could be described as an independent expenditure campaign on Trumps behalf, according to the House Permanent Select Committee on Intelligence. Furthermore, an attempt to further a broader Kremlin objective: sowing discord in the US by inflaming passions on a range of divisive issues by weaving together fake accounts, pages, and communities to push politicized content and videos. Furthermore, to mobilize real Americans to sign online petitions and join rallies and protests. Wikileaks had published many documents which revealed some very vulgar language attempting to link an allege pizzagate pedophile ring conspiracy surrounding the Hillary Clinton campaign. These accusations were later deemed as fake news by mainstream media although 28-year-old Edgar Maddison Welch drove from North Carolina to point a firearm in the direction of a Comet Ping Pong restaurant employee here in Washington, DC.

Artificial Intelligence Disconnect

Fast forward to Wednesday, November 1, 2017. The Intelligence Committee Hearing with social media took place on Capitol Hill with representatives from Facebook, Google, and Twitter. The companies were ready to answer the pressing Congressional questions about the full extent of Russian use of social media. Why did it take them so long to discover this abuse of their platforms, and what do they intend to do about it to protect our country from this malignant influence in the future?

Beginning the hearing with prayer possibly was the perfect way to start for the social media companies and the Committee. All of America's social media technology giants had an opportunity to clear their minds- and get ready for sworn testimony in this unclassified matter of discussion. Bearing in mind during the hearing that free speech is guarded by our Constitution, many of the social media companies did not want to infringe upon their users' rights. All three companies acknowledged they understood the magnitude of the events which have unfolded, and on a scale from 1 to 10, with 10 being the highest level of understanding.

Sean J. Edgett, acting General Counsel for Twitter acknowledged and stated during his oral testimony "Today, we intend to show the Committee how serious we are to addressing this new threat by explaining the work we are doing to understand what happened, and ensure that it does not happen again." He expressed how any activity in unacceptable and that take the responsibility, currently detect more than 4 million malicious account a day. Twitter has created a dedicated team within the company to enhance the quality of information their users see and block malicious activity whenever and wherever they find it. The company continues to aim at being a safe, open, transparent, and positive platform.

Moving right along with the oral testimonies to accompany the written testimony, Mr. Colin Stretch, General Counsel for Facebook stated "at Facebook our mission is to create technology that gives people the power to build community and bring the world closer together." Mr. Stretch also expressed that people expect authentic experiences to share and to connect. Facebook acknowledged that fake ad accounts violated policy and were removed. They plan on making a significant investment by hiring more ad reviewers, doubling or more on their security engineering efforts. Putting in place tighter ad content restrictions, launching new tools to improve ad transparency and requiring documentation from political ad buyers. Facebook plans to expand efforts to work with law enforcement and are building more AI to help locate bad content and locate bad actors. Hopefully Facebook will add a face lift to their leadership and bring more than 2.3% of African American employees on board.

After Twitter and Facebook gave oral statements, Google didn't decline their opportunity, and Mr. Kent Walker, Senior Vice President and General Counsel of Google stated "Google believes it has the responsibility to prevent misuse of their platforms and take responsibility very seriously," and recognized the importance of the Committees mandate. Google has agreed to safeguard against these attacks in the future with building industry leading security systems and recently they launched their safe browser system. They are aware of attempted attacks to manipulate their systems and have since secured spam and security measures on its YouTube platform ensuring that no view counts or number of subscribers are inflated. Google now uses fact check to help user's spot fake news on Google News.

Now that the social media companies acknowledge their wrong in the role Russians played on their platforms, hopefully they will implement policy and procedures to ensure that these fake ad accounts are not created.

Update: A day after the #TechHearing a Twitter employee is fired for deactivating the account of President Donald Trump.

Positing Your Company to Sustain this Digital World

The weather was fitting for the *"Digital Transformation Summit"* which was powered by Dell. The summit took place at the Ritz Carlton on Thursday, October 26.

Power On

While standing against the wall, scanning the gigantic ballroom for a seat; I'm thinking to myself- not many people declined the opportunity to learn from Dell. The *"Digital Transformation Summit"* started on time, with the first panel discussion *"Transformation from the Hill."* Remarks given by Congresswoman Robin Kelly, (D-IL). The next panel discussion *"Realize Your Digital Future"* was presented by Marius Haas, President and Chief Commercial Officer, Dell EMC.

Upon my arrival, *"Workforce Transformation Chat"* was about to begin. Moderated by Steve Harris of Dell EMC. During this discussion it was refreshing to learn that Dell does listen to its customers. Panelist Randy Kendzior emphasized that point by sharing a story about one of his clients, the military. "Chrome based system had a glare, PG took it back and turned into a black matte-based system that we have today."

There's a possibility learning and listening about technology can be a bore, but when Dell presents a summit, it's a dynamic experience and lives up to its title, *"Digital Transformation Summit."* From the Technology Expo to the digital character drawings; the summit was centered on innovation.

The next panel *"Cyber Security from the White House"* was presented by Grant Schneider from the Executive Office of the President. Mr. Schneider shared some service provider expectations with participants.

"Our technology has to be simple, and apple did this well" he stated while given remarks. Not only that, but the service must have tools that are agile- solve next week's issue, having integrated tools which work seamlessly with tools already existing. The one expectation which was most valuable he mentioned – service providers having tools that are affordable.

Along with securing the systems out the box, making them easier for consumers.

Summit Highlights

With more than 25 panelists on the agenda scheduled to talk technology, writing a few notes down while listening is helpful. Here are some tips that can possibly help your company in this digital world:

Believe it or not! Companies must create the culture to sustain its current mission to align in this digital technology world. Not talking about being left off *"Bad and Boujee"* Culture, but tech culture. In doing so, companies should consider **adapting** to the tech environment, positioning themselves for **advancement** in the environment, along with **flexibility**; being able to solve existing, pending, and future issues in the technology world.

First, a company must *think* of the culture it wants to create in this technological world, but *security* is key. The goal is to preserve the company's culture in this technological world. How will you ensure that your company can exist beyond its domain name? Can it survive Cyber security threats?

Then a company must consider its look. That is correct! No culture of people wants to look displeasing. In other words, will your company have a local office or remote location? Currently, many employees in the federal government have the capability to tele-work from home. Not only that, but what will the culture of the company look like? Will you optimize your existing value or contract for hire specific tasks?

Although artificial intelligence is taking over, companies should not solely rely on AI alone. The companies feature should be vast and wide, however align with the mission of the company which can sustain in the tech world.

Perhaps you're a legacy company transitioning into the technology world. Don't freeze up!

You can create a culture within the existing company! But before you embark on the transition, *research* is key in securing your data:

- Companies should consider researching the current and future threats in the marketplace.
- What current software programs best suited for the transition?
- Who are existing service providers?
- What type of network system updates will be required?
- Evaluate company value, current and future.
- If legacy company, how many employees have information technology experience or educational background knowledge? How many are you willing to train?
- Are employees comfortable with the transition tools?
- How will the creating the culture impact the company? Both positive and negative results are important.

Now the most important question at this point could possibly be how your company will survive. By first establishing an identity worthy of sustaining a culture in the technology world. In an environment where identity is king since it is data, the company's infrastructure depends on its first security measure. Keep in mind that you want your company's culture to sustain Cyber security threats.

Hopefully, these tips can help jumpstart your company's transition into the digital technology environment. The shift takes time, but technology is constantly changing so don't wait too long to create a sustainable culture in this technological environment.

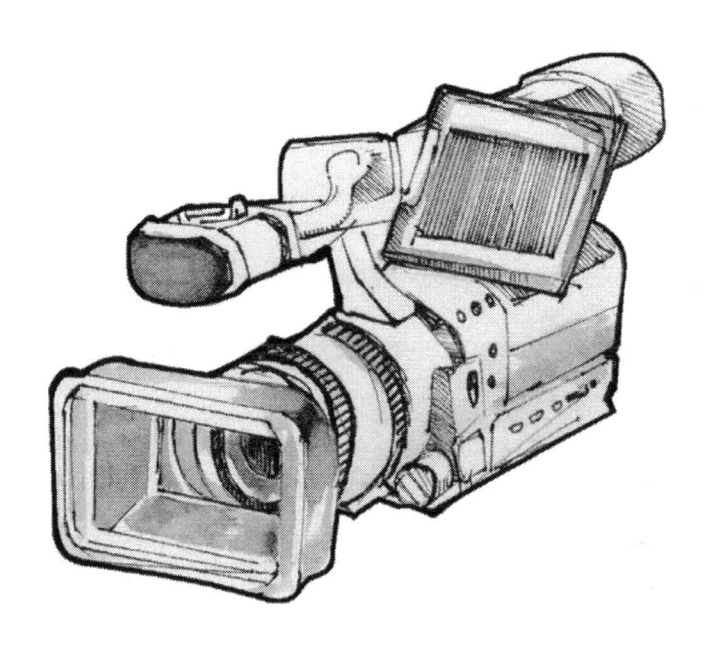

Title: The Glitch v. The Gag

Interactive Source: Vimeo.com

Original Production Year: *2017*

MJ News Update: Not sure traditional or legacy media news station were anticipating the drastic change in news consumption but the transition has arrived and it's here to stay. While attending the University of Louisiana my video production class contributed to a focus group study of synergy in the news with new technology being the center focus. Now many years later, I am able to contribute to creating the content to sustain the digital era. Pretty incredible

The Desk Is Dusty in This Digital Media Era

Recently, a manifesto or memo was released on Twitter generating much buzz. The memo agenda was centered on "gender identity" and company culture. And in no time causing a catastrophic controversy. The 10-page report analyzed genders and how they correlate in the company culture. In a world of tech, which we currently live in, who doesn't know how to send an email these days? Even President Trump tweets! Being a journalist it\'s important to remain unbiased and factual at all times in your reporting. Since the news has spread, and it's both-sides to a story, it was very peculiar that this manifesto has generated so much buzz after this, which leads me to question the nature of the minds of the people working for the tech Giant. Tune In

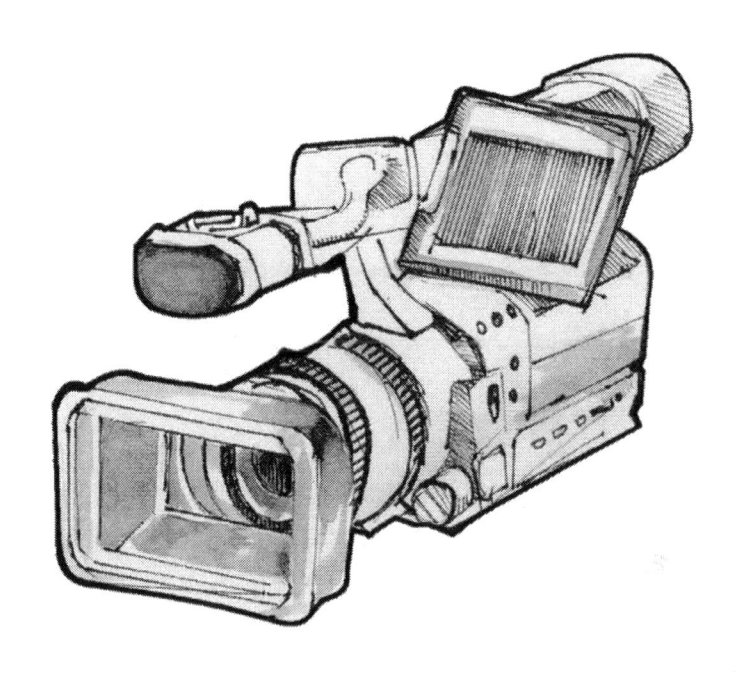

Title: When the Press Link Up Social Media Conference

Interactive Source: YouTube.com

Original Production Year: ***2016***

*****MJ News Update:*** **This was truly a remarkable experience. The power of bringing innovation together to learn, share, and grow is a once in a lifetime experience. This conference afforded the opportunity to bring rising entrepreneurs in the digital creation market together in Washington and it was a success. In fact, I am led to believe this conference influenced many in Washington, starting at the US Copyright Office, along with President Donald J. Trump who hosted a social media conference at the White House.

Tools for Social Media

It was a beautiful August afternoon at the University of the District of Columbia Student Center, as the decorations went up in preparation to kick off "When the Press Link Up" social media conference presented by PR WIZ, LLC. The purpose of "When the Press Link Up" is for social media enthusiasts and entrepreneurs to gather, network, and learn through educational workshops taught by top industry professionals with the goal to enhance current skills awhile embracing new ways to creating compelling content.

"When the Press Link Up" special guest presenter included the US Office of Copyright providing vital information for social media enthusiasts and entrepreneurs to aide with securing content through copyright along with fair use of content.

Tools and Tips for planning a conference using social media

- *Brainstorm*: think about what type of conference you want to plan (music, social media, sports, festival) why are you planning this conference? Who will attend this conference? How does the guest speaker's & presenters align with the conference theme, purpose, or goal? What type of venue should be used? Who will attend this conference? Will you need volunteers? Will you serve food? Will you have promotional material? What does your budget look like?

- *Create*: a conference title & make sure it\'s catchy, attention grabber.
- *Develop*: a logo which could be used interchangeably, something which will generate a buzz, comments can later be used for testimony. Along with creating any videos or pictures to enhance viewership of event post and attract potential attendees.
- *Engage*: others in the conference by gathering email listings, consider Facebook friends objective is to inform the public that the event exist.
- *Gather:* invitation listing with prospective event attendees in mind. Start in your gmail account then

work your way to your Instagram, Twitter, business cards, ig.

The tough decision comes in as to which tool is most cost effective for promoting your conference. Using your personal or business social media platform to promote your event is standard, moreover maximizing the medium is key. The purpose of "When the Press Link Up" is a social media conference it was best to utilize a social media advertising company. Now the benefit to using this method for your social media profiles gain followers and event interest instantly which is great for your event. The downside to using social media advertising companies is that in the event a protest suddenly erupts chances are it will overshadow your promotion, such as what "When the Press Link Up" encountered during the Alton Sterling protest in Baton Rouge, Louisiana.

Now it's time to integrate all of your final plans & strategies along with social network platforms to execute the action plan. Planning 150 days prior to your proposed scheduled event helps ease anxiety and allows flexibility. Leveraging social media is key and finding the perfect balance of content will help keep your social media platforms balanced and help manage content.

Plan with Purpose

Proceeds from "When the Press Link Up" will be donated to a deserving Arts and Humanities student attending the University of the District of Columbia, along with Teach for Madagascar education nonprofit organization. Here is a recap of this amazing social media conference "When the Press Link Up."

Fresh Start for the FCC

Greeted by *"don't censor our internet just cause Trump sucks," "FCC hands off the internet,"* I attempt to make my way into the first Federal Communications Commission meeting under the Trump Administration.

New Commission Chair

At the last Commission meeting, Chairman Wheeler couldn't wait until the clock struck
12:10 p.m. so he could officially be out of office. Who wasn't in a hurry is current
Chairman Ajit Pai. My arrival was timely, considering it was just in time for press questions. But before we present our question, other members of the press asked Chairman Pai about set-top TV boxes, net neutrality, and what he thinks of internet companies. Here's what I think of Internet cost, if it makes any difference, $1,000 is too much money for fiber

optic service! Needless to say, the cost of cloud space has been altered by climate change, maybe.

Q & A

DC Voice: *Does the FCC plan on extending its jurisdiction beyond news stations to video online streaming?*

FCC Chairman Pai: *That's an issue that we haven\'t taken a look at in the last week, can't make a comment at this time.*

Towards the Future

Well, I do recall the time my colleague presented on the topic of net neutrality in 2010, and it sure has generated much buzz since then. Perhaps the FCC will take its own advice regarding staying connected during these digital times and extend its jurisdiction regulations to online video streaming sources since networking platforms now have the capability to go LIVE. Facebook introduced LIVE with future plans of taking it up a notch, creating room for competition in the online video streaming marketplace.

Not sure if this is an entryway for more fake news or room for competition, either way it is beneficial for the user of the platforms. In the event that you\'re watching Facebook TV and a closed captioning is misleading, who will be accountable? Currently, not the FCC. The company must acknowledge the error if any. After all, closed captioning isn't to mislead any audience, it is for the hearing impaired to have access to the medium.

Whether it's a TV Station or Facebook TV, regulations still need to be in place.

Title: EVERFi and FISLL Lead the Way

Interactive Source: Vimeo.com

Original Production Year: *2018*

MJ News Update: Being on time is beneficial when you want to get an interview. It's not guaranteed but, being on time does assist in the possibility of landing one. I was able to interview the NBA- All Star Mr. Allan Houston. The most memorable moment was being able to see the excitement on the youth's face and how they engaged at the museum. An inspiring production!

EVERFi and FISLL Ignite the Digital Era Launching FISLL 306

While many tech start-ups are seeking capital to introduce their plans, EverFi has joined forces with FISLL to launch FISLL 306. FISLL 306 is designed to teach students to think critically about their own personal legacy by exploring the lives of pioneering African-

American throughout history. This interactive digital program was inspired by Allan Houston's FISLL brand, which focuses on the tenets of faith, integrity, sacrifice, leadership and legacy.

The launch took place inside the spectacular Oprah Winfrey Theater at the Museum of African American History and Culture. Although Oprah wasn't in attendance to hand out great gifts, NBA All-Star and founder of FISLL Allan Houston gave jewels of wisdom- sharing with the students of Digital Harbor High. Houston offered "You pick your battles, but leadership is inside all of us." The students were inspired by

Mr. Houston's words of wisdom. His University of Tennessee college professor Dr. Cynthia Fleming, told the students "concentrate on the kind of education that will allow you to fit in this digital society where you are."

With much wisdom, encouragement, and inspiration, students of Digital Harbor High were ready to embark on a journey at the museum of African American pioneers who have contributed so much to the fabric of America. This tour was designed to enlighten the students of what they to can accomplish through hard work, sacrifice, and integrity. And to teach the students that everyone is a leader and can build upon their legacy.

Caption This? Modernizing Wireless Phone Text Compatibility

While the rest of the world is either going LIVE on Instagram or Facebook all at once, the Federal Communications Commission held its last meeting under the Obama Administration led by Chairman, Tom Wheeler with a favorable motion to support real-time text providing reliable telephone communications for Americans who are deaf, hard of hearing, deaf blind, or who have a speech disability. Before his January 20th departure, Chairman Wheeler thank the staff for their hard work, and dedication to increase digital age accessibility, affordable broadband regulations while helping more people stay connected.

All in Favor

With the favorable majority vote, and request for editorial, phone companies will now have to replace telephone text support. It's out with the old TTY, and in with the new support for real-time text aiding Americans who are deaf and hard of hearing, deaf-blind, or who have a speech disability. Commissioner Rosenworcel says at the meeting "the future belongs to the connected, and the FCC extends that connection to more people." The real-time text would allow natural conversation, communicate quick and efficient, use in the event of emergencies and the purchase of specialized equipment isn't needed. Now let's review this plan which AT & T petition asking the FCC to initiate a rule-making that would authorize the industry wide substitution of real-time text to meet accessibility requirements. Maybe Sprint will acknowledge the petition but implement a petition of its own since they have proposed to bring 50,000 jobs to America under the new Trump Administration.

Although special equipment isn't needed, will the wireless phone carrier adds a special tax onto the customer's bill for this real-time text service? Will the customer need to increase their data plans for real-time text? Furthermore, these are questions for the Trump Administration to tackle. Chairman Wheeler expressed his gratitude for being in his position and looks forward to his resignation by 12:01 p.m. on January 20th.

Much uncertainty roamed the room of the Commission meeting, moreover, rest assuredly, take a deep breath, the work will be appreciated is the belief one of the Commissioners has. Despite Chairman Wheeler applauding one of his staff for their ability to deliver internet protocol, or counsel on delivery and determine what it should look like, he doesn't know who should deliver protocol or counsel closed captioning for online streaming companies, although many Americans consume alternative news from their wireless mobile devices.

The Uncertainty

TheDCVoice: *At the present the FCC does not have jurisdiction over video programming that has not been shown on tv, will the FCC extend its jurisdiction to digital online media with regulations on closed captioning?*

FCC Chairman Wheeler: *that's a question I'd think you'd have to ask the next administration*

Perhaps this is a question for the new Administration as the Chairman stated, or a case for the DC Circuit court, caption that? Moreover, who will be accountable for the accuracy of the closed captioning once implemented for real-time text communication?

Credibility in a Trend and Thread Society

The American society has advanced to the point of no return, literally! Just think of all the #trends and #hashtags you encounter daily? Not to mention the new wave, artificial intelligence. If all of this vanished, what would the people do? Many would most certainty miss President Trumps tweets about his plans for America, along with his ongoing struggle to clarify communication with the "fake news media."

The Missing Thread

When trends and threads lead the way in any society, there are many possibilities for "fake news" this and "fake news" that to surface. Especially when anyone can create a profile, blog, or website. Nonetheless, the truth shall set everyone free- besides news reporting is supposed to be unbiased, fair, balanced, and factual at all times; this could ultimately be where the journalist credibility lies.

Let's go back a few #trends, #threads, and #hashtags to figure out where did the "fake news" derive from. Was it #HillaryClintonEmails, #Pizzagate, #ImpeachTrump, #FindOurGirls, or #NotMyPresident? Perhaps it began during the Presidential campaign trail? That's when alleged emails surfaced containing information about Hillary Clinton's campaign manager John Podesta and child sex trafficking. Which supposedly took place at

Comet Pizza on Connecticut Ave in DC. Or maybe it was after Edgar Welch, 28 from North

Carolina came to DC on a mission to with a rifle and a revolver to "self-investigate" #Pizzagate. Furthermore, some extensive investigative journalism can reveal the missing threads.

If I recall correctly, Hillary Clinton denounced the "fake news" during her campaign run. Then talks and rumors of Russia interfering in the Presidential election circulated the internet. After that; the demand for President Trump to reveal his income taxes started to trend, then he wins the election. Despite the wiretapping of a private conversation in which then "business mogul Trump" is saying "grab em by the pu**y." President Trump has been conducting himself as a commander-in-chief, and with over 100 days in his position, he hasn't made an attempt to tweet any tax information.

While the American people wait for the grand reveal of President Trumps tax information, Facebook has since capitalized on the "fake news" trend implementing and establishing its "content clearing house" agency. With connecting over 1 billion people, Facebook is reaching beyond the threads creating employment opportunities for over three thousand individuals to classify and determine news credibility. Perhaps this will aide in President Trump not banning press from the White House.

The Content Controversy: Who knows How to Ad?

The way in which we communicate with friends and family on a daily basis has changed since the telegram. Not to mention a telephone booth. Television has also transitioned from the black and white 1960\'s Zenith wooden box TV set; to the consumer telling the remote to change the television channel. Furthermore, the way consumers consume content has changed tremendously.

Money, Power, Respect competition in the marketplace

When you turn on the television, there is now a variety of programming to select from. With the added luxury of paying a cable TV network service provider for additional channels expanding beyond the plug in antenna with high definition and color. Not certain if variety was thought out strategically by mainstream media generals, nonetheless we can now program the television set for a later time to watch a show. Television advertisers sure didn't have a diverse target market back then, or understand their audiences purchasing power, but they knew "blacks" would be willing to spend on goods and services.

The variety of TV programming has changed since "A Different World." Audiences didn't have the access to tweet Whitley Gilbert and Dwayne Wayne a response to their relationship issues, or interact with the cast of the show like "Watch what happens Live with Andy" on Bravo. Moreover, there are a variety of ways in which a person can consume programming such as a smartphone mobile device, tablet, laptop, or desktop computer. Looking back to my undergrad years, at the University of the District of Columbia in 2010, the media industry has taken a major shift. Newspapers were not printing many volumes, website developers were highly sought after. And news anchors were being laid off in part due to the variety of news sharing sources such as blogs and bloggers. Other factors that impacted the industry shift such as independent media, and proximity.

With the introduction of the online content streaming and sharing service provider YouTube, it has enable independent media to leverage the use of social media tools to deliver programming at a much rapid rate, cost effective, and to a large audience locally and globally. This innovative way to deliver content to consumers proved to be most effective until 2016 when the content monetize feature created room for competition to exist in the marketplace. Who says competition can't exist in the same marketplace? Mainstream media possibly since they want all the advertising revenue and the audience too. Well guess what, you can't have your cake and eat it too. Maybe mainstream is having a challenge leveraging the new medium, but independent innovators managed to launch channels with no problem until apparently advertiser had a challenge aligning content with a friendly ad on the streaming service.

Have you not seen any over sexual advertisements lately that weren't friendly for your child during a television program commercial break? Did you call the television network to complain, or stop buying that over sexual product? No. The online streaming service didn't have any issue with finding ads featuring Goldman Sachs transporting pipes for content conveying to an audience about race. Or featuring an ADD medication during content, encouraging people to vote as the appropriate advertisement for the content. Since when did consumers care if the ads and the content aligned? If that is the case some markets are reporting false data.

This battle among the mainstream media generals and independent media has been a constant one and is heating up causing financial hardships on innovative content creators. Someone isn't generating the revenue that has been projected in the data, and now the innovators have to suffer. This is not fair to freedom of the press, but perhaps Facebook will be the ultimate media clearing house for what constitutes as credible news and what ads match the content, what editorials need edits so forth and so on. I'm certain the Associated Press didn't factor this method into journalism standards and will have to update their books to feature Facebook fake news versus real news.

IBM is Helping Move Government and Industry towards a Digital Transformation

Whether you're looking to take your business up a notch with cloud space coverage, Cybersecurity solutions or ensure the product sourcing through blockchain technology, IBM continues to provide the innovative solutions both government and industries need to thrive and carry out their mission, shaping the future of government and industry. IBM held its second annual *think Gov.* on March 14 at the Grand Hyatt in Washington DC. A moment of inspiration, insight, and perspective from eminent speakers and presenters from both government and industry sharing the art of the possible with technology, demonstrations incorporating AI, open scale, blockchain, cloud, quantum and the internet of things.

*A few **notes** gathered from the experts at the second annual think Gov. Event*: **Using Data to Achieve Success**

- Tools to discover information have gotten better.
- Artificial Intelligence will assist in having conversations to accomplish a task since a lot of information is unstructured.

- Start small then go big. People tend to think about the big solutions, but start small building on that success.
- Artificial Intelligence can help government and industry professionals understand their questions in plain language.

Improving the Work Experience with Digital Platforms

- Changing composition in the workforce by shifting culture in organizations and how they think and use technology.
- New technologies help shape products and services for government and industry use.
- Understanding Cybersecurity is not enough to improve business process and exchanging information.
- The supply chain getting beyond the fisherman test, blockchain is more integrated and improves security- allowing limited ability to alter records.
- Focus on data that your agency or business can really modernize. The most important jobs will focus on data.
- Your agency or business success rate starts from a concept.

Keynote Session *with John C.P. Allessio, Vice President Global Services, Red Hat*

- Red Hat is here to assist customers with today\'s digital transformation by providing specialize and custom tools.
- Recognizing a number of customers and products going through a large change trying to go digital, a tool which Red Hat provides, Dev Ops can help power company's digital transformation, through their unique application and method of infusing culture, operation processes, and technology to provide meaningful solutions.
- Red Hat offers open invitation labs, where they share with customers the methods and tools necessary to assist your organization on their journey to digital transformation.

Where Does the Value Lie: In the Institution, Student or Debt?

In a few weeks from today, many people will embark upon a new journey, or some will be back in the swing of things completing their college course curriculums. Nonetheless, where does the value lie in the institution, student or student loan debt?

Asset Breakdown

The institution is simply a building without administrators, faculty, facility teams, and students. Suppose the value would be in the property of the institution in this case. In Washington, location is everything! Let's examine the value of assets further. What will keep the operation and beautification of the building? That's a two part answer considering the facilities team would beautify the building, and students keep the operation of the building functioning.

There is a possibility the institution uses its discretion when inviting its prospects in for admissions. An added pitch would help boost the prospective student into signing that promissory note to remain in that building for the duration of the study agreement requirements. Once the building breaks down into departments for degree studies, it allows for additional cost to accrue allocating that expense to the prospective student. The student must then determine if these fees are reasonable for the resources offered.

Using the University of the District of Columbia as an example of institutions with resources because it serves as an urban land grant institution. The Land Grant Act of 1862 granted land to each state in the union for the promotion of education in agriculture and the mechanic arts. The university has a farm, along with Water Resource Quality Center for the District and beyond making the resources very plentiful.

Value Place Holder
Moving right along with our value assessment, now it's time to determine the value of the student in the institution. The first observation and conclusion of this assessment is that

the student's value is priceless, so we really don't need to go any further. But to be fair, the student's asset contribution equates to culture, diversity, academic strength, with the will to learn what it takes to be successful in their prospective career paths. Those are just some surface value assessments. If we go beyond the surface assessment, we learn that added cost are attached to bringing added value into the institution, so therefore it is beyond a mutual beneficial relationship.

Maybe it is the security that cost the most while in an institution setting. The possibilities are plenty, but the student is a major asset beyond the liability of student loan debt.

Student loan debt is scary, so perhaps there is much value in fear or the recent computer glitch wiping out $5 billion dollars of student debt is friendlier. Quite frankly, the loan service doesn't share in the same sentiment. Needless to say, if you must pay your way- it's best to pave the way in the process to securing that promissory note ensuring that your time was worth the value at the institution.

The Worth

Most institutions don't understand value outside of the student's account number was the sentiment shared by Rodney Sampson, Chairman of TechSquare Labs during the *"Rethinking the Investment Game: Angels, Incubators, Accelerators, Crowdfunding, and other Alternative Capital Sources,"* panel discussion at the MMTC 17 Conference. How devastating, luckily for platforms such as the MMTC Pitch Competition, former or current students can take their professional careers to new heights with prize money of $5,000 dollars.

<u>MJ News Update:</u> Moment of honesty. I filed a civil complaint against the US Department of Education. Furthermore, for some suspicious and strange reason the filing didn't reach the US Department of Justice so the courts closed the case. It was after this filing I kid you not that the Biden-Harris Administration would piggy back off my action and suggest student loan debt relief. I'm not sure if I will be eligible now that I brought froth action, but it didn't get far in the proceedings. Meanwhile, the cost of higher learning is outrageous when some people just watch YouTube all day and learn from those channels.

Keep It Simple, Central, and Smart, Access to Procurement

In a marketplace where technology drives the bottomline, operating a business can have its patterns of ups and downs. But what really drives the business operation crazy is when it's a challenge accessing the data.

System Error

Can you recall how many times you've been ready for business and can\'t get into the system because of a password? It left you feeling perplexed, and wondering if you made any modifications to the account access information. Or what about the times you\'ve applied for small business loans, or grant opportunities and the information isn\'t easily accessible and all over the place? That leaves room for a missed opportunity.

Granted Access

If you operate a business in the District now or in the future, you have a greater chances of doing business here. The plan is for more accessible in part to the "Accessible and Transparent Procurement Amendment Act of 2017," introduced by Councilmember Kenyan McDuffie, Chair of the Committee on Business and Economic Development. This bill would streamline the procurement process, increase transparency, and increase competitiveness in contracting by increasing the number of bids received. It would also require the District government to place all District government solicitations over $25,000 on a single website that provides machine-readable and searchable information. Furthermore, Executives must post a list of all contracts in the preceding year that had a closing date less than 30 days from the date of issuance.

"Additionally, posting the list of solicitations with closing dates of less than 30 days will enhance transparency and ensure that residents can easily learn about the justification for contracts with extremely fast turnaround times," stated Councilmember McDuffie. Under the current procurement method, District government has the potential to waste taxpayer dollars.

Title: Electric Tour Pops Up in DC

Interactive Source: YouTube.com

Original Production Year: ***2018***

<u>***MJ News Update:***</u> It's always remarkable to see the growth and development of brands and ideas when you have had a conversation with the person behind the innovation. I am very proud of these ladies and just how far they've come and so much growth and development along with sustainability in a every so changing market.

Online Merchants are mastering the Marketplace

It was a vibrant Sunday afternoon in the District for the Electric Tour Pop up Shop at Maketto on H Street.

Customer Connection

The Electric Tour Pop Up Shop featured top e-commerce businesses such as GrayScale, Unicornuniverseusa, and local business GLOSS. Online merchants have managed to connect beyond the computer orders placed by their customers. The benefits of having an online business are booming these days. Infusing the pop-up trend provides an innovative shopping experience for both the customer and merchant. The pop-up trend gives the merchant an opportunity to interact with their customers. And the customer can meet the face behind the computer screen.

Online Merchants Market Data

From the market data, despite the projections- many millennials have ditched standing in the long lines at the mall and opt for a more intimate, face-to-face point of sale, which has much more added value. It looks like these merchants are managing to stay in the marketplace. With reasonable price points, you don't have to stress about going over your budget at the pop-up shops. Here is a tip: it's best to attend the pop-up events because better deals are present. Customers could get 2 pairs of trendy frames for $20 bucks, which is less when clearing out your cart online.

So, I think it's safe to say that pop up shopping is here to stay!

Chapter Four: Culture

Cultural Heroes help keep art and culture alive in The District

If you haven't noticed by now, Washington, D.C. is very vibrant and eccentric. Rich in culture and heritage; not simply because of Congress. But the main contributors to upholding the culture of D.C. are Washingtonians. Often the nation's capital can get confused with Capitol Hill, but the city has its own governing body consisting of a mayor and city council.

Some of the most critical components to preserving the US Constitution are held here, upholding the laws the rule the land. There are over 600,000 Washingtonian's who live beyond the jurisdiction struggles of federal government and the district government. Many demonstrations take place in Washington, so it has a very symbolic and prestigious presence being felt. As Congress holds true to voting on the floor, many Washingtonians want to preserve the rich heritage and powerful culture of the people post implants and gentrification.

With a current 20-year Comprehensive plan in place to beautify and modernize the DC; what was the reconstruction plan back in 1968? On April 4, 1968, many had received the devastating news that civil rights leader and activist Dr. Martin Luther King, Jr. had been assassinated. This was the turning point in which the city would feel the people\'s pain both literally and physically. Not sure if holding onto those memories make the occurrence any different in measuring pain then and now, but what was the district like in 1968? Sure, no Lyft to get you from U street to your home. There was racial tension in the air due to prior injustices in America regarding African Americans. Who was Mayor back then? Walter E. Washington. He was appointed the 1st Mayor-Commissioner of the city, and Walter E. Fauntroy was first Vice Chair of the Council. What was the education system like along with the true climate in the city during the 1968 Riots? The film "1968 The journey Fifty Years Later," gives a depiction of those questions during that time.

DC Community Heritage Project presented its 12th Annual DC Community Heritage Project Showcase held at Charles Sumner School on September 11. The preservation of culture is important to any community. It allows for a better definition and understanding of history. D.C. is more than government and the rich arts and culture that have magnified and made and tremendous impact on the city. Stories like "dc 1968," presented by Dr. Marya McQuirter, contribute to keeping the legacy alive. "dc 1968," is a digital storytelling project about Washington, DC during the entire year of 1968.

The project moves beyond the hyper-focus on the uprising after the assassination of King and amplifies the art, activism, architecture and every-day life that made 1968 such an extraordinary year in D.C. Through its mission and dedication, DC Historic Preservation Office assists in facilitating the importance of culture preservation. "It's through educational outreach and community engagement that allows for avenues of preservation," said State Historic Preservation Officer David Maloney.

All district residents can continue to build upon those legacies by discovering "culture heroes." Who are they? Ask Joy Ford Austin, Executive Director Humanities DC. In her call to all, she expressed that" culture heroes" must be culture conscious of the city, using culture to advocate for DC residents. Ward 5, you heard the call, are you a "culture hero" keeping art and culture alive in the district?

Have You Noticed How Well Trees Treat Us?

When was the last time you took a look at a tree? Sure there is a smartphone app to teach you how to garden, but when was the last time you took a good look at the trees in your community? The old cliche' "Tree of Life," holds some truth and value. The tall wood plant provides food, furniture, products, oxygen, healing, and a home to a number of species on planet earth. Trees have an intricate and vital role to play in our ecosystem. Some trees tell stories whether it's of the civilization or the climate. The tree bark can reveal much on the outside, and inside of the tree.

This weekend I visited the U.S. National Arboretum. It is a breathtaking beauty. Filled with trees, floral plants, shrubs, and nature's species – butterflies, bees. Established in 1927 by an Act of Congress, the Arboretum is on 446 acres of land with 9.5 miles of winding roadways.

You don't need to have any interest in being an environmentalist or botanist to consider visiting the Arboretum; a hidden gem in the district. It only requires some comfortable shoes, water, and a camera to capture the beautiful scenery and just take some time to bond with nature. I forgot to mention, it's free, so you can't go wrong. In fact, it's the perfect first date. Don't have to spend any money, and you'll get to spend time enjoying the beautiful scene; even if the conversations doesn't seem to be going anywhere.

Could you imagine for one second what the world would look like without trees? Just about everywhere you look, you can spot a tree. We sure wouldn't have heard the cliché "the grass is greener on the other side." Many paintings have illustrations of trees or flowering plants. The trees bring an element of calming and protection into the picture or atmosphere; suppose this is where the role of oxygen comes into play.

Have you ever notice which trees attract certain species? Or even considered which trees are responsible for producing the fruits, nuts, and plants that we need to sustain life. Better yet, how which bark provides health benefits. Don't think of a tree like a block chain process, but think about who planted the tree? How long the tree has been alive, and what can the tree produce? These are all important questions and help with understanding the true value the tree holds to the environment and the community.

What is building or creating a sustainable life without being surrounded by trees? Not much breathing room for growth perhaps. But take some time to think about how well the trees have treated us, and what we can do to help them stay alive, while they sustain our lives. Here is a start, simply enjoy these patterns of the tree bark. Take a moment to examine how they are similar, different, and the colors. Are all the patterns the same? What do they say about the climate in that environment? Don't wait until the treeing for construction projects to care.

Title: Show Off and Turn On Your Summer Sexy

Interactive Source: YouTube.com

Original Production Year: ***2018***

MJ News Update: This production really made me proud! I was able to elevate my engagement and reach along with secure major sponsorships and collaborations. Wellness is really important, and I did appreciate everyone's help in making this event a success. The information that was shared along with learning new exercise techniques. I'm looking forward to doing something like this again in the next city that I relocate to.

A Sizzling Summer Fitness Boost

It was an exceptional Sunday at City Pop Dance in the District. Starting the summer with a sizzling fitness boost of motivation and inspiration. "Show off and Turn on Your Summer Sexy", a spectacular Women's Wellness event, exercising with Crystal Wall of MixFitz Studio in Houston, Texas. Along with some great health tips and information provided by Dr. Ijeh.

Bringing her Southern hospitality, style, and own fitness flavor, Crystal Wall has returned to Washington, ready to empower women through fitness exercise that is fun. Adding some southern spice and flavor to your workout. More than exercise dance movements, "Show Off and Turn On your Summer Sexy" was an opportunity for women to learn some important health information and tips from Dr. Ijeh, a Naturopathic Doctor. Dr. Ann Ijeh is Owner and CEO of Asa Health Network. The Asa Health Network recognizes that each patient is unique and pledges to deliver patient-centered care. Asa Health Network's goal is to provide the highest quality of healthcare using minimally invasive, natural, and nontoxic treatment modalities.

Through Dr. Ijeh's presentation, participants were able to learn the importance of "health is wealth" along with which foods help keep the body functioning, and what is required to help maintain those bodily functions.

Furthermore, Dr. Ann Ijeh emphasized the importance of water intake, and how with age our body's ability to retain water starts changing. So, hydrating is very critical. With special thanks to Essentia Water, event participants were able to Show Off, Turn On and hydrate the Essentia way, improving people's lives through better rehydration. After an intense fitness exercise, Essentia was right on time, for overachievers.

According to the survey, some "definitely" enjoyed the experience, "absolutely" enjoyed the experience, and added, "yes, please have another one" when asked if they would attend another event powered by the GAIL Movement. When asked if they feel better after attending "Show Off and Turn On your Summer Sexy," the response was "Yes! I feel energized," "so much better." A great way to start your Sunday with an added Summer fitness boost and health tips. To learn more about the Asa Health Network please visit their website.

A Refreshing and New Season: Springtime

With change comes some adjusting. Who isn't ready to see some beautiful Geraniums, Canterbury Bells, Carnations, or prickly Rose bushes? I can sure use some consistency with my outside Vitamin D intake directly from the sun, so that alone makes me ready for spring!

I'm looking forward to planting a few seeds and watching them grow. Along with looking at nature's beauty from a different lens, a digital camera. As you all know, I aim to deliver the best to my audience, always providing captivating and compelling content, organic and fresh. Recently, I purchased my first digital camera in time for spring – and its part of the Canon family.

Although I took photography in high school and college, I've never owned a digital single lens reflex camera (DSLR). My style was more catered to a manual single lens reflex camera (SLR) moving towards the nearest darkroom for a hopeful development to appear. So long to the numerous expensive sheets of photo paper, and making sure the right amount of light has hit the paper to develop the film.

Well, this will be a new learning process for me and I have my student hat on, ready to take in all the lessons. My very first lesson came from bringing the digital camera back to Best Buy because my images were appearing too dark. I was under the impression the film speed determines the grain of the image. However, in this case, I needed to adjust the ISO speed to see the beautiful images. After that quick lesson, I went into practice mode.

Here are a few of my practice test shots. Let me know what you think! They're not Cherry Blossom program cover ready just yet, but I intend to capture nature's beauty! Don't forget to smile if I see you!

Let's Spring forward to a great season!

Title: Team Gary Russell Ready for Barclays Center

Interactive Source: Vimeo.com

Original Production Year: ***2018***

MJ News Update Ahead of the January 26 fight night at the Barclays Center in New York City, The DC Voice had an opportunity to talk with Team Gary Russell before they entered the ring.

Title: The First Friday of 2019

Interactive Source: Vimeo.com

Original Production Year: ***2019***

MJ News Update: I wanted to do something different at the start of the New Year. However, one of the contributors who just arrived at the online publication thought it would be a great idea to start my year off with a 2015 re-entry story, and I did object to it because it's my content, and that wasn't how I wanted to start 2019 digital news off.

Title: Jack & Jill Journey to Recovery

Interactive Source: Vimeo.com

Original Production Year: ***2019***

<u>MJ News Update:</u> Attending a movie premier in DC is a lot of fun. The best way to ease any anxiety is write down all of your questions before hand so once you reach the red carpet you're ready to ask the cast questions and keep it moving to see the movie premier. As a journalist you must find a formula that's fitting for your style of reporting.

Urban Movie Channel Premier Subscription Streaming Services Presents Jacqueline and Jilly

On Monday night, it was time to roll out the red carpet, and head to the Lincoln Theater in Washington, DC for a star-studded premier of *Jacqueline and Jilly,* an original series presented by premium subscription streaming service UMC (Urban Movie Channel), Days Ferry Productions. *Jacqueline and Jilly* is a portrait of three generations, two shattered dreams, and one accidental addiction. When the daughter of a privileged political family develops an addiction to prescription painkillers following an unfortunate accident, it goes unnoticed by those around her. As the problem becomes more apparent, the family must face the truth about addiction and each other while banding together for the sake of their daughter's survival and recovery.

Be sure to catch up on the recently premiered original series *Jacqueline and Jilly* featuring

Victoria Rowell, *Executive Producer and Director*, Daphne Maxell Reid, Nikko Austen Smith, Charmin Lee, and Lamont Easter. New episodes of the original miniseries will air weekly through January 10, 2019.

The Black Family Business – Ben's Turns 60

Originally Published February 2, 2016,"The Black Family Business"

Back in 1958, August 22nd to be exact, the sweet melody and sound on the Saturn II jukebox could well have been "I want to stop, and thank you, baby," as Ben and Virginia Ali opened the nation's now famous Ben's Chili Bowl.

More than just chili and cheese, Ben's Chili Bowl served a very prominent and classy close-knit community. Located in Washington, D.C., on U Street in the Northwest quadrant of the city Ben's Chili bowl is surrounded by some of the most iconic theaters such as the Lincoln Theater and Howard Theater not to forget The Republic and Booker T. During the late 1920s U Street was known as the "Black Broadway" because of the very progressive entertainment and dining at restaurants with white tablecloths.

Blacks in business during the 1950s were faced with challenges due to racial inequality and lack of cultural understanding. Along with overhead costs operating a business comes with investing not only money, but time, sacrifice, and dedication. For the first twenty years through all the social and economic changes happening, Mrs. Ali was working longer hours since she only had one other employee at the time. Mrs. Virginia says "it was very hard on me because there were no streets, no subways, and the property tax had increased."

Although some businesses didn't welcome people of color other than to make a purchase, Ben's Chili Bowl welcomed everyone from its opening day in 1958 until today. It is the most racially, culturally, and economically diverse thriving business in the city. In the 1960s some areas in the district were ravished by riots and engulfed in flames following the assassination of Dr. Martin Luther King, Jr. Many businesses had a curfew. However, Ben's Chili Bowl remained open, and it was the actual meeting place for the city police and other officials to come together to figure out a plan to end the riots and violence occurring in the District.

Because of its location and one-of-a-kind chili half smoke you would often find influential

African Americans such as Bill Cosby frequent Ben's Chili Bowl. Mr. Cosby dined at Ben's

Chili Bowl where he ultimately meets his love, Camille. Bill Cosby would turn down press conferences at the Press Building and conduct press conferences at Ben's Chili Bowl instead.

Family has always been at the forefront of Ben's business plan which contributes to its thriving business, and almost fifty-seven years later Ben's business hasn't slowed down and Mrs. Virginia Ali says "having two of my three daughters-in-law running the business with me makes it very special."

MJ News Update: There's beauty in writing a beat story. However, it's rather upsetting when someone steals your content and plaster it on their website as if they're the original writer of the article. I remember it like yesterday having to send an email to a website because they had stolen this article and no given me credit. I'm an American journalist and I don't play behind my work. I will check you if need be.

Title: Who's the MLB All-Star Fan?

Interactive Source: YouTube.com

Original Production Year: ***2018***

MJ News Update: Baseball is a big deal. It's America's favorite sport. Its three strikes and you're out. The Major League game is huge and it happened in DC. The pre-game was pretty cool also. I wanted to learn who the biggest fan in attendance was and I found some amazing youth.

Major League Baseball's First Base are the Youth

Take me out to the ball game! Not just any ball game though – the Major League Baseball All-Star game! The 89th All-Star game is scheduled to take place on Tuesday, July 17th at the Nationals Baseball Park Stadium in Washington, D.C. The diamond field at the National's ball park will be glittering in platinum, or dusting some fans in disappointment; nonetheless batters up!

Whether it's first base, second, third, or hitting a home run, baseball has been the great unifier and equalizer in America. Despite the racial tension in the country during the 1920's and 50's baseball found a way to accommodate both racial ambiguities from Babe Ruth to Hank Aaron. It was those early transformations to the sport of baseball that made an entryway for the sport to be integrated into the school system. It was eventually offered as an extracurricular activity. At one time parents were able to complete an application for their child's participation in sports programs at the facility. Exposure to baseball as a youth is very important to its preservation.

Perhaps more recreation centers in the cities could offer baseball as a weekly or monthly activity. Especially for those youths who are less likely to have exposure to the sport. Most often recreation centers in the cities encourage exposure to football rather than baseball. Maybe it's more cost effective. Depending on which school children attend, baseball is often an extended extracurricular activity. I recall not being exposed to baseball until middle school where I was the manager because my batting skills were not of a certain standard.

According to Commissioner Manfred for Major League Baseball, "youth programs are important, it's about our future." So after the All-Star game is over the engagement of exposing youth to baseball is still an urgent need.

Moreover, now is the time for the best of the teams in both leagues to gather their top nine players to play in the 89th Midsummer Classic in D.C.

Title: Being ready is real when disaster strikes

Interactive Source: YouTube.com

Original Production Year: ***2018***

<u>MJ News Update:</u> Having to prepare for any storm is scary. You want to make sure that you have access to all your essentials but then it seems like you've missed something. Since this article was written, Congress did fail on its oath by neglecting the people who have been affected and impacted by Hurricane Helen. The response effort was that the Federal Emergency

Management Agency (FEMA) had no more revenue to render relief efforts during the 2024 storm season.

Being ready is Real When Disaster Strikes

When disaster strikes, simulation and training are over; it's time for action. No one anxiously waits for a disaster to occur but we know all too well that one day a disaster will arise. Being ready is real! The National Health IT Collaborative held a congressional briefing, co-chaired by Congresswoman Stacey Plaskett *"Disaster Preparedness: Building an Innovative National Response Network in Underserved Communities"*. The briefing focused on lessons learned during disasters. It examined disaster responses and the need for better awareness and preparedness.

Most people have the common emergency response items in their home. Typically, a fire extinguisher or first-aid kit to care for a minor cut or burn. These are great tools for emergencies within your control. What happens when you need medical attention, food, and shelter? Who will supply the aid to the affected area then? Who will be responsible for covering the cost of the aid? It's then that you must think about all the key players involved in disaster relief.

These are general questions that become very complex and critical when disaster strikes. Waiting to the last minute could be a very hard lesson. Furthermore, in the event first responders are needed on the scene, the time can take longer than expected for rescue. Most response times in under-served communities are delayed, which present constant barriers to addressing needs during a disaster. The infrastructure in under-served areas tends to give in much faster during a disaster.

Under-served communities are often the hardest hit during a disaster. They are usually the last to be repaired. While on travel to New Orleans, I rode the bus down to the lower 9th Ward. During Hurricane Katrina, the lower 9th Ward suffered the most damage, displacing hundreds of thousands of residents. Thirteen years later, it still looks like a hurricane passed through – just after you bypass the Brad Pit Housing Project. Repairs during a disaster can take anywhere from 10 days to thirteen years. It can take that long when you consider the efforts of the response team and coordination with government officials to ensure that resources are released in a timely manner.

On the bus, I learned that families had been separated to seek medical aide. A husband and wife were waiting on their roof for a helicopter to rescue them from the flood waters that had reached their attic. The husband ended up in Oklahoma while his wife went to Texas. Many people were given the opportunity to return and rebuild their communities, but many declined.

As New Orleans continues to rebuild and people still consider returning to the city, many other states and territories must begin the rebuilding process. Texas from Hurricane Harvey, California wildfires, and Puerto Rico along with the U.S. Virgin Islands, must start building new infrastructure that will endure the next disaster. *"What infrastructure is disaster ready,"* Dr. Lynda Chin of *REDI* stated during the briefing. This time around the goal is *"build as it should be"* says Mr. Godbout, *NHIT Care Campaign*. The community should return to something better.

A critical part of infrastructure is the ability to communicate during a disaster. First responders in Puerto Rico were presented with a major barrier for communication – a failed power grid. Not everyone has access to a generator. This is when a backup communication plan is critical to help combat prolonged emergency care and better assess people who are potentially in danger.

Coordinating all these efforts requires a strong and very smart team. There are critical components in disaster preparedness. Always keep the community's needs first. Being ready is real when disaster strikes. Often some lessons are learned the hard way and can have a major economic impact and causalities. So, learning the best practices for prevention of a catastrophic situation is a must.

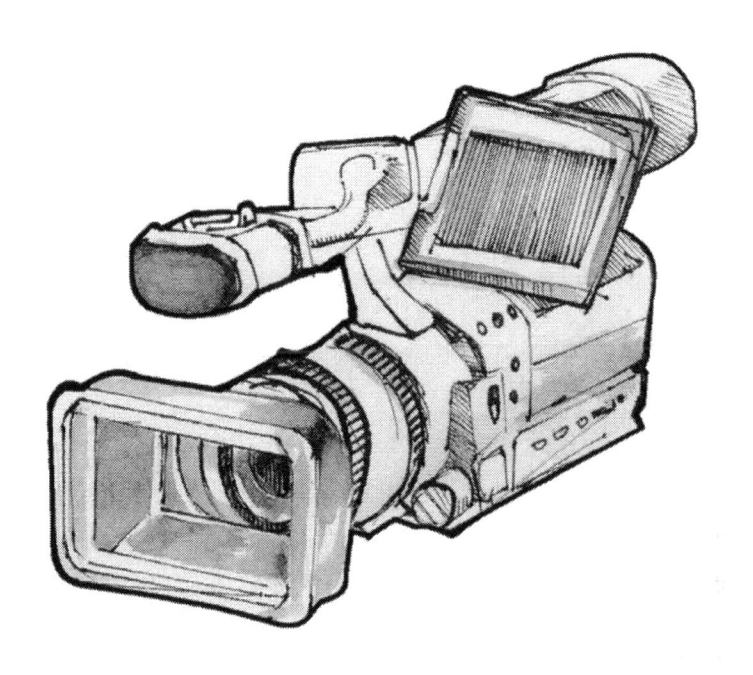

Title: Trill Grill Fest takes over DC

Interactive Source: YouTube.com

Original Production Year: ***2018***

MJ News Update: An experience is what I always want to share with my audience and as long as the atmosphere affords for that then that's what is created. Having some really cool moments that's not always planned according to a storyboard is great because you can expand your creativity.

Trill Grill Fest takes over D.C.

The summer is off to a scorching start in the district. However, the people didn't allow the heat to slow them down. More than 3,000 people came out to support the Trill Grill Fest. What do you bring to the Trillest BBQ of the summer? Surely, your favorite bottle of water, a towel, your ticket, and Trill Grill Fest takes care of the rest. With a star-studded lineup including Big K.R.I.T, Bun B, and Translee, supporters withstood the scorching heat. The games were on deck for the Trillest BBQ, from cards to Flip Cup Champions reclaiming their titles. Many gave the mechanical bull a ride for one trill time.

It was certainly the Trillest BBQ of the summer, see for yourself.

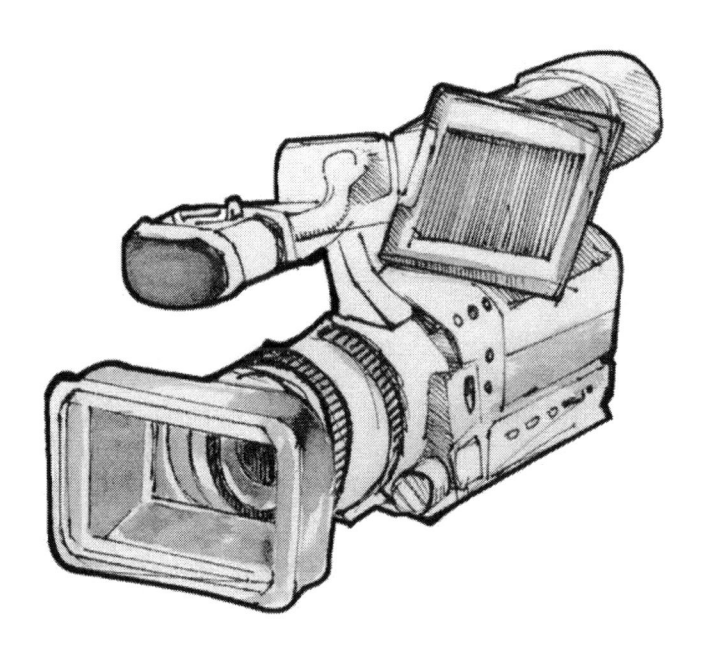

Title: Fight Night at MGM National Harbor

Interactive Source: YouTube.com

Original Production Year: ***2018***

<u>***MJ News Update:***</u> Boxing can be a brutal sport so knowing how to report blow for blow is a bonus. This is probably the most intense reporting ever because you can't take your eyes off the ring. One opponent might have a jab or knock-out before the 7th round so you have to stay ready.

Russell Still Reigns as World Champion

The signs were everywhere that Saturday's fight night was in full effect. Even the parking garage was packed to capacity, with cars creating parking spaces along the wall. From parking level P6 – take the elevators to level C for entry into the MGM National Harbor for the main event, Gary Russell, Jr defending his WBC Title Championship against opponent Joseph "Jo Jo" Diaz, Jr.

At the time of my arrival, Cobia Breedy from Bridgetown, Barbados was in the ring against opponent Christopher Martin from Chula Vista, CA. I was rather impressed with Cobia's performance in the ring considering that I missed his last fight at MGM. Not only that, but during the media day workout his had to find his pace and momentum on the frog exercise equipment which made me think about his movement in the ring come fight night. Breedy's shots landed him a victory. Some of the power packed punches landed on Martin even caused him to stumble a little. Cobia gave himself a C for his fight, however I disagree with that.

He deserves a B- for his precision of punches landed during the 6 -round bout. Cobia's coach says "time to step up."

It was during Cobia's interview that I missed Gary Antuanne Russell's Junior

Welterweights fight. When we last spoke, nine days before the fight, he stated that he trains for 12 – rounds. Although this was a 6- round bout match, Gary Antuanne ended the boxing match in round two, despite his opponent Wilmer Rodriguez from Santo Domingo, DR being overweight.

The action doesn't end there! In fact, it was time for Gary Russell, Jr. to take to the ring defending his WBC Featherweight Championship title in 12 rounds against Joseph "Jo Jo" Diaz, Jr. "Jo Jo" made his way to the ring on the tune of Migos – "Walk it like I talk it," but the crowd remixed the song adding some "boos." The sounds from the crowd changed from a remix version of "Walk it like I talk it," to cheering on Gary Russell, Jr. as he made his way to the ring with a little Curtis Mayfield – "Keep on Pushing." Both songs brought forth an extra boost of energy to ease any anxiety because it was about to be SHOWTIME.

From the first round bout, the jabs were jarring, and jaw dropping, there were moments "Jo Jo" wanted to attack Gary's body, breaking it down to secure the victory. It was then in round three or four Russell hurt his jab hand, but still had to use it. "Jo Jo" appeared to have a strategy of cornering Russell Jr. to get a knock out, but luckily Gary got from out of that trap. "Jo Jo" says Gary Russell, Jr. is very quick and he thought that the slip was a knock down. It was truly a gladiator fight, blow for blow, with not all of the jabs landing as precise as either boxer may have wanted it, but Russell stills reigns as World Boxing Champion defeating Joseph Diaz, Jr. in 12 powerful, body blow rounds- finishing with a score 111 to 117.

Title: Cypress Hill Cannabis Clouds

Interactive Source: YouTube.com

Original Production Year: ***2018***

<u>MJ News Update:</u> The National Cannabis Festival is always a great time. Being able to capture the experience has been the most enjoyable. My first credit for using content in an advertisement came from the NCF so I appreciate their recognition of my work and giving me credit.

Cypress Hill, Cannabis Clouds, and Cool Weather: It's Time for A Celebration

If the cliche' *"three times is the charm,"* holds any truth, then the National Cannabis Festival was certainly, without any doubt the place many truly wanted to be this past weekend. Not many missed the memo for inviting consumers interested in the cannabis culture, who like attending concerts in wonderful weather conditions, while learning in one central space. There were so many people that I'd lost count after entering the festival. The obvious catch is that the National Cannabis Festival has created a campaign that is here to stay beyond the smoke in the clouds at RFK Stadium on this past Saturday.

What began in 2015 as an idea when a small group of cannabis enthusiasts who joined together around the idea to create The National Cannabis Festival – an event celebrating progress on marijuana legalization in DC and across the nation. The founders envisioned a festival recognizing the spirit of the cannabis movement and the non-profit groups that have fought for so long to end marijuana prohibition. From the first 5,000 in attendance back on April 23, 2016 to over 10,000 this past Saturday, April 23, 2018. The National Cannabis Festival has attracted people from the District, Maryland, and Virginia to the shores of Mississippi, Ohio, and Atlanta.

With a star-studded lineup consisting of the likes of Cypress Hill, Back Yard Band and many more artists, many festival goers were looking forward too much fun. For some it was their first time attending the festival while some are continuous supporters sharing the sentiment of enjoyment from their expressions. Many of the first timers said they would consider coming back to the festival. Not sure how many strains of marijuana I encountered, moreover it was a great learning experience. Tune in…

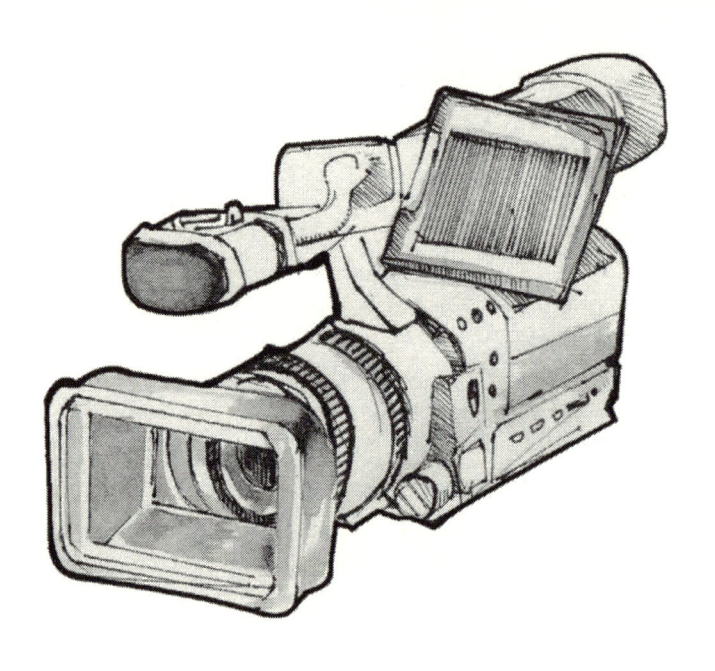

Title: The Crescent City New Orleans

Interactive Source: YouTube.com

Original Production Year: ***2018***

<u>MJ News Update:</u> Let the good times roll is the philosophy to adopt when you visit New Orleans, Louisiana. This production is very special because it captures the true essence and culture of the city, the people. People are what make a culture thrive and sustain it. The city has not been the same since hurricane Katrina which displaced so many people from the city and the lower 9th ward has yet to be revitalized. However, it remains the top tourist destination of the US.

Title: Black History Month is American History

Interactive Source: Vimeo.com

Original Production Year: **2018**

MJ News Update: History is an account of an event, and depending on the motives and intention of the writer some parts can be left out or embellished. This is why it's imperative to learn oral tradition also. The concept of

Black History has been distorted throughout the US simple because the account has left out something critical for the reader to consider and most often it's the starting point. If American history is supposed to be colorful then why is everything always black and white? The spectrum of colors in a rainbow don't ever get carved out into its history. Knowing where you came from is a great way to keep your history alive in North America.

Black History Month Continues Because It's American History

As Black History Month makes its exit to stage left, will #Wakanda live forever? Only time will tell, however the Black Panther movie is making much money. Did the movie make up for the 28 day celebration of Black History Month? Not quite, but it is certainty on the verge.

Will people still be eager to educate themselves on the contributions which blacks have made in America after today? Perhaps. Although, we acknowledge the contributions of blacks during one month out of the year, Black History Month is American history. Sort of separate but equal. Similar to the conditions of the blacks in the South. Separate in the aspect of access to quality living standards beyond the slave quarters and cotton fields.

Furthermore, equal in the essence of living beings.

Let's not limit our learning to focus groups along with case studies. From time to time they can lack all the elements to bring forth an accurate analysis. And don't just learn about Dr. Martin Luther King, Jr. He is America's favorite somehow, but there are plenty more great contributors to America who are black. Frederick Douglass came long before Martin was thought of. In fact, about 200 years ago, Frederick Douglass was born and would later bear the name "Lion of Anacostia." If it were not for the contributions of blacks in America where would our nation be? Who would cover the Capitol? Who would have done the hard labor low-wage job?

The celebration is over, but the learning can continue.

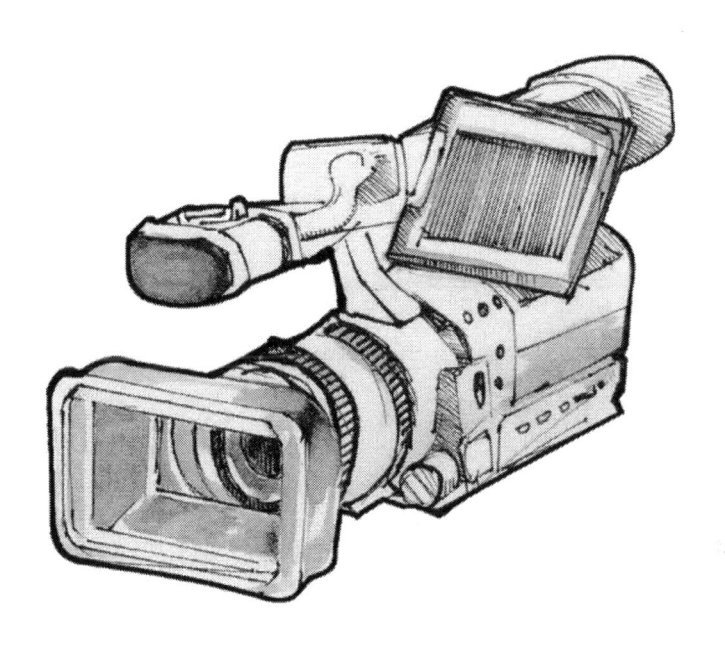

Title: Black Films during Black History Month

Interactive Source: Vimeo.com

Original Production Year: ***2018***

<u>MJ News Update</u>: Representation matters in everyday life. Without it, some people can often feel as if they don't belong. Being able to watch a film that captures the essence and beauty of blackness is very beautiful and needs to be broaden. Certain films document the culture, heritage, history, and lifestyle of a people that don't gain worldwide notoriety so Black Films are a bonus enriching the culture.

Black History Month Film Festival

During Black History Month, Mayor Muriel Bowser's Office of African American Affairs and

Urban Film Review presented the *"2018 Black History Film Festival."*

There's a possibility that if blacks in America are educated about Black Films along with Black Film Directors during the month of February while honoring Black History Month, they would most likely retain the information. Maybe it gives more meaning and purpose to a group of the American population who are most likely rejected from recognition during the remainder calendar months.

The idea along with the potential for a black American film maker to break the box office during the 1920's was simply a wish on a paper perhaps. Ready or not "Shuffle Along" came right on time. Although it's a musical, it was a body of work co-written by Eubie Blake. Moreover, the first

Broadway Show written, produced, and performed by blacks. Only if Vimeo, or Kweli TV were accessible and available back then? Maybe more blacks would own more movie production studios along with distribution companies, and the copyright.

Luckily the times have changed for the better. Today, filmmakers don't have to wait on anyone else direction but their own. This gives them the creative freedom of expression in their body of work. It also allows a cost-effective distribution method. Many black creatives, no need to mention a specific category have been swindled out of their body of works. Or paid a non-desirable and decent living wage. Currently, comedian, talk show host and actor Mo'Nique has asked for her supporters to stand with her to boycott Netflix. She believes the earrings are not sufficient or compliment her resume. She reassured her supporters "I love us for real" during her protest.

Black Directors today, have the ability along with access to tools – to make a quality and desirable motion picture, documentary, or short film worthy to be featured during the Pan African Film Festival or even the Black Film Festival in DC. Does having access readily and available translate into a tremendous film? Not necessarily, the quality needs to be worthy of watching. During the DC Black Film Festival held at the Lincoln Theater, film Director and actor Tim Reid suggest anyone can make a movie, but "the quality of the work has fallen." Moreover, one of the panelists speaking about *"Business and Legal Aspects of Filmmaking,"* suggested in unstructured situations you must create structure, set up a system.

Title: Celebrating Frederick Douglass during Black History Month

Interactive Source: Vimeo.com
Original Production Year: ***2018***

<u>***MJ News Update:***</u> It's very dynamic that we don't get much information about Frederick Douglass as Martin Luther King, Jr. especially when the context of the conversation is reparations. Douglass was against slavery so any institution or organization which still functions under such umbrella or associates with elements should be brought to the light. Perhaps we can discuss more of Douglass than Martin when freedom is the goal.

Celebrating Frederick Douglass during Black History Month

Would it be best to reclaim the entire month of February, and celebrate Black History Month in March? Maybe that is asking too much. Well, considering we are approaching the twenty-eight-day mark, it is wishful thinking. However, before the end is near let's honor Frederick Douglass.

Known as *"The Lion of Anacostia"* Frederick Douglass was born 200 years ago in 1818. Married twice with 21 grandchildren it was a need to purchase the 10 acres of land and 5bedroom house with an attic.

While traveling, Douglass's travel-trunk signified his wealth. Perhaps he would travel to see his good friend Susan B. Anthony. Along the way, Frederick gains an interest in Women's Rights – and they are reaching their full potential.

Is Black History Month Still Appreciated or Declining in American Value?

From the recent Kente cloth adorned along the shoulders and neck of Congressional Black Caucus Members during the State of the Union address to the discovery that Britons may have been black 10,000 years ago, is #BlackHistoryMonth still appreciated in America, or does it no longer hold its value?

Just think for a moment. How would Carter G. Woodson feel to learn that his dedicated studies towards preserving a culture of people; who have contributed to the fabric of this great nation has been given the extended honor of a hash tag? Now let's celebrate #BlackHistoryMonth. It will be as instant as a Google doodle with a little hopeful intelligent fact.

Where is the real honor with giving much more recognition than a generated hash tag to celebrate Black History month?

Is the honor in the same commercial sound bites that haven't had a fresh voice over in the last 20 years? Or is the honor in the recent tweet by the NAACP "Mae Carol Jemison an American engineer, physician and NASA astronaut? She became the first African American woman to travel in space when she went into orbit aboard the Space Shuttle Endeavor on September 12, 1992," #MakeHistory #BlackHistoryMonth. This is a much better phrase along with distribution method to get a few facts out there to the public. Perhaps some effort is better than no effort at all. Considering how these trends come and go, Black History Month hash tag is sure on decline these days.

Why do we even recognize Black History Month in the first place? Possibly because a great American writer with a focus on blacks in America wanted the contributions of the people to be recognized and celebrate much more than their tribulations; when they were transported on slave ships to the "New World." So, in 1926, Carter G. Woodson established Negro History Week. Before Negro History Week, in 1915 he founded the Association for Study of Negro Life and History to encourage scholars to engage in the intensive study of the black past. Prior to this work, the field had been largely neglected or distorted by the hands of historians who accepted the traditionally biased picture of blacks in American and world affairs, according to Britannica.

How is it that blacks are always asked to attend an assembly gathering, but barely get any recognition? This was quite evident at the recent Grammy awards during Kendrick Lamar acceptance speech. He had to ask the audience to "give it up for Hip Hop." In a different setting, many are getting ready to gather at the movie theaters to see Black Panther, starring an all-black cast. There is so much excitement about the movie during the month of Black History, one young lady has a tweet which has amassed 125,000 views of her dancing "showing up to see the movie Black Panther like this! – followed by a fist pump emoji and video camera emoji #ImBlackandImproud #BlackHistoryMonth."

Maybe this is the way the culture celebrates now. Just with a little-known doodle fact, a few hash tags by civil rights organizations, along with a dance for a movie during the month of Black History. Well, there are about twenty days or so remaining. Hopefully, someone will keep the honor alive beyond a hash tag. Senator Tim Scott did post a rare Black History Month fact tweet "Today is the 50th anniversary of the Orangeburg Massacre – a tragic and pivotal day in the fight for civil rights in South Carolina #BlackHistoryMonth."

Title: Don't Need to Gel

Interactive Source: Vimeo.com

Original Production Year: *2018*

MJ News Update: "Don't Need To Gel" is generating much buzz around the internet since its release. "Don't Need To Gel" was inspired by America's Tech giants that are very innovative and leading the world of artificial intelligence. Reporter Mindy Jo wrote the song and her alter ego "MJ Tha Great" laid down the versus. Believe it or not I used my Samsung smartphone device to record my smash hit song. It was as though I was in the fancy studio and had a handkerchief over the microphone and started going in as if I was a pro!

Hillary Clinton Honors White Women with a Bash during Women's History Month

Is it proper etiquette, for a former First Lady and Secretary of State to travel the country talking about her short-lived sitcom of sharing the exact seat of her husband, by bashing women to persuade the people in the audience? Maybe this is a new strategy for a political party to adopt to prevent the possibility of any future alleged meddling in Presidential elections.

During a recent private visit to India, former Secretary of State Hillary Clinton attended a panel discussion at the "India Today Concave 2018." She was asked about the outcome of the 2016 Presidential election results to which she replied *"We don't do well with white men, and we don't do well with married white women. Part of that is because of the identification of the Republican Party, and a sort of ongoing pressure to vote the way that your husband, your boss, your son, whoever believe you should."* Should she have just spoken in first person instead? Who is we? Is she referencing the Democratic Party? Was there extra pressure on her to win President?

Is now a great time to shift the blame on women who identify as white in America? Should this be considered pragmatic principles, or the sub-conscious calling for clarity on conceding to the 2016 Presidential race? Was her response a strategy to instigate or inflame the decisions for white women in future elections? Should the families in America figure out who really is making the best decision for the welfare of the whole family? It sure doesn't appear to be white women, according to the election poll results along with how Hillary feels.

Are African American women left out of the conversation because they don't identify as having a partner or husband, a son, or a boss who believes that they would have a change in heart in their living conditions and standards? Or are no African American women affiliated with the Republican Party? Was Hillary Clinton's statement the perfect stage setting on a global scale to bash white women, but have the perfect public relations pitch when she returns home and gathers with African American women?

Chances are the conversation took place after Hillary Clinton slipped down steep stairs in India during her private trip. If so, that may have had an impact on the inference which was made. But that could very well be her own personal sentiment. Since Bollywood is home to India, it would have made more sense to have a conversation centered on her #Grammys presentation of "Fire and Fury." But that was not well received either, maybe that was because of white women also.

Sure, many women around the world will remember former First Lady Hillary Clinton especially during Women's History Month, and how she ridiculed them on a global scale. Such a grandiose sentiment to send during a moment of celebration and honor. Hopefully, her panel discussion did not spark the need to spread a division among those who identify as women, regardless of their ethnicity. Maybe she encouraged more women to think independently from those whom believe in them when making sound decisions. Can women think for themselves during election time without the pressures of the men in their lives? Hillary Clinton may think differently, hence her now global campaign for not conceding to the 2016 Presidential elections.

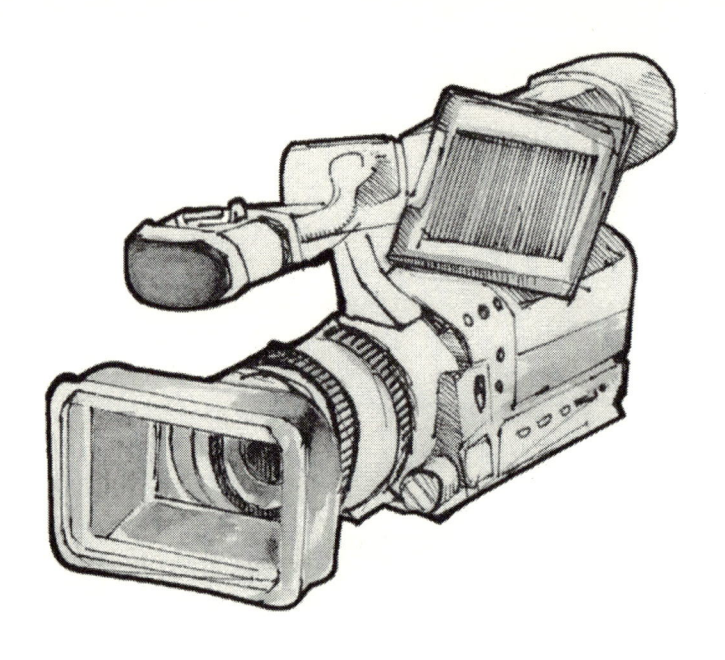

Title: A Hot Day on the Hill

Interactive Source: YouTube.com

Original Production Year: ***2017***

MJ News Update: Capitol Hill has a culture of its own and they have a different attitude and outlook of the world. Some of our most precious laws originate from there and they don't always have the best interest of the people. Furthermore, if you bring forth your grievances just hope the crowd conducts themselves in a civil matter.

Bring America Back to Life

Today could've well been "Heart Health Awareness Month," because the hearts of America and American's were on both ends of the spectrum on Capitol Hill this morning. From either direction, the megahertz was unleashing at a voltage not sure the current broadband system or healthcare system could handle.

Need Lifeline

The Healthcare bill needs much resuscitation at this current moment. But before that happens, emergency disaster teams and doctor's need to be able to communicate with one another to save American's- especially those in rural areas. It will be a shock to learn who will be saved first and with fair treatment.

While waiting over 65 minutes, my heart certainly had time for the uncertainty which was inside the Energy and Commerce Communication and Technology Hearing room in the Rayburn Building. Off the record- it was worth the wait. However, not sure how much longer American's can wait on a healthcare bill which allows for decent medical treatment coverage. Nonetheless, it will be pleasant to learn when the FCC will extend its jurisdiction beyond TV programming with particular regards to regulations for online streaming closed captioning, along with the enforcement of more diverse and positive media platforms.

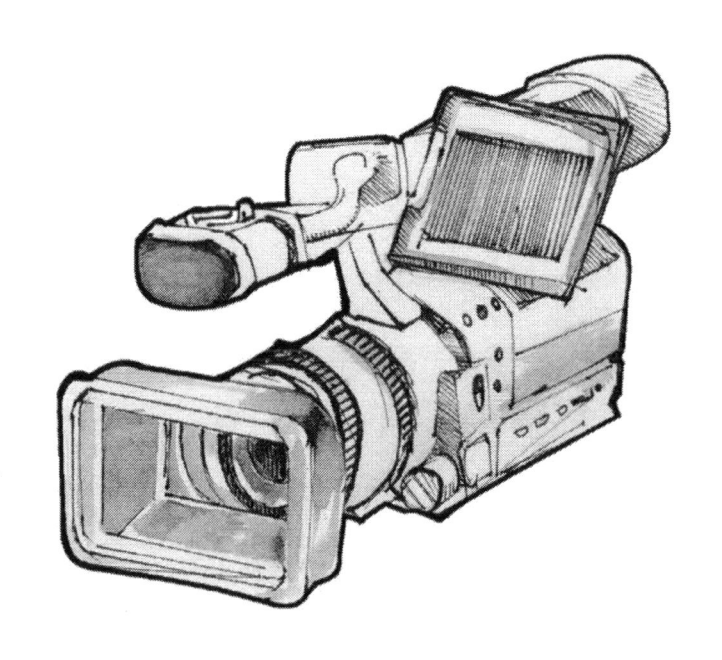

Title: The DAMN Pop-Up Tour Stops in DC

Interactive Source: YouTube.com

Original Production Year: *2017*

MJ News Update: In 2024, Kendrick Lamar let the world know "They not like Us." That statement did resonate on a grand scale especially during a time where the culture of Blackness has been adopted and made a mockery of allowing anyone to claim such identity even if it's the Vice President. Kendrick also made headlines for his 2025 Super bowl performance. Many critiques believed that Lil Wayne should have been headlining it.

The DAMN Pop-Up Stops in DC

Someone get TOP DAWG on the line – it's a heat wave in Washington, but it won't stop the Damn Pop- Up held on Friday in Georgetown at UBIQ clothing store. Not sure how humble you can be in the scourging heat, blazing the beautiful people in line. Not sure if anyone was able to sit down though, perhaps they would just stay hydrated.

The Compton California native Kendrick Lamar brought the West coast heat to the DMV, heating up the streets in Georgetown hours before the night's concert at the Verizon Center. No matter the weather, Kendrick Lamar has dedicated fans who will support. The lines were wrapped around the corners with a guy telling the crowd "please don't block the business's doorways." While many anticipated his arrival, many fans were just excited to experience the Damn Pop Up in DC. Tune in.

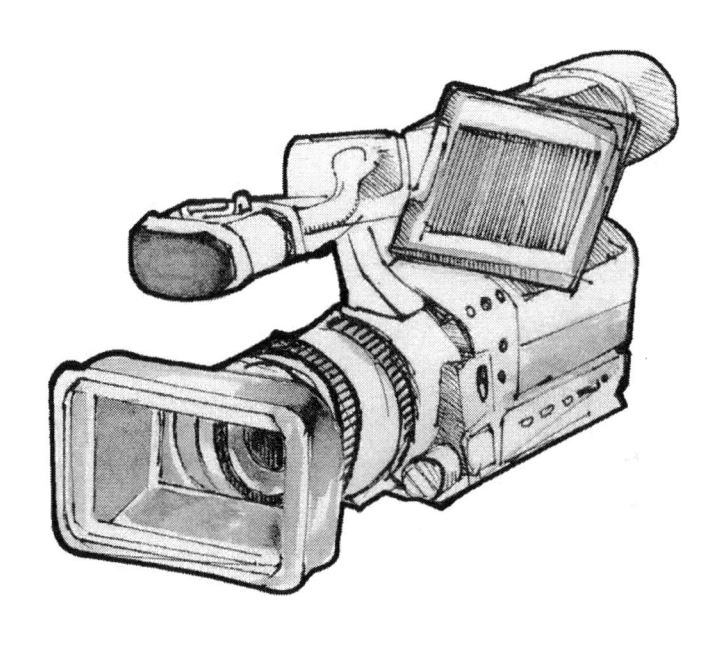

Title: The DC Voice, Day 1 at MMTC Conference

Interactive Source: YouTube.com

Original Production Year: **2017**

MJ News Update: Some people can be very rude at panels and that's just their nature. That's all I can express about this production.

The DC Voice Attends MMTC 2017

It was a hot Wednesday morning for the Multicultural Media, Telecom and Internet Council 15th Annual Access to Capital and Telecom Policy Conference held at the Westin Hotel, in Georgetown. Once inside, the start of the panel discussions cooled off the crowd.

Talking broadcast media in an era of "fake news," not to mention infusing tech talk in the discussion, with added access to capital can be challenging. Day one at the conference, considering the weather was great. The panels were very informative, and off the record, I attended many discussions without much information to build upon, so this was rather refreshing. Take a look.

Title: Issa wave GAIL movement on the move with ISHTALK TV

Interactive Source: Vimeo.com

Original Production Year: **2017**

MJ News Update: Getting Active is Life! A great way to start your fitness and wellness journey. Nothing worth having comes easy but once you see the results it's so beautiful. The movement has since elevated to Getting Active is Love and it shows by the way you care for yourself.

The G A I L Movement Connects with ISHTALK TV

Powered by PR WIZ, LLC, the **G A I L movement** is an exclusive *Fitness, Lifestyle, and Wellness* online resource facilitator and connector. "Getting Active Is Life" ™ is taking over the web at a moderate rate, generating much buzz, and interest. Creator Mindy Jo had the opportunity to share the movement with ISHTALK TV.

ISHTALKERS TV discusses topics ranging from social and political issues to tabloid and celebrity news, sex and relationships, love and games, hosted by AJTurnup, Bmore, and Champagne301 on Wednesday nights at Ripped Radio Network, an online entertainment network.

What is the GAIL movement? That is a great question! A movement focused on promoting engaging in physical activity by adopting a healthy lifestyle, nurturing the Mind, Body, and Soul.

Title: The Time has Arrived 4:44

Interactive Source: YouTube.com

Original Production Year: ***2017***

MJ News Update: This production was very different and I wanted to infuse some different elements in the experience. It appears I did just that because Sprint was inspired by the production. The store was very crowded and the people enjoyed their time. Hip Hop has since been around for 50 years now. It's remarkable to see the future of Hip Hop and those who have paved the way for the genre of music to thrive worldwide.

Its 4:44, Time to Wake Up

Perhaps if Prodigy was still physically present, he could enlighten us as to which rapper is more conscious Kendrick Lamar or Jay Z. 2Pac could be considered also, but not sure it would be reasonable since Jay Z makes recent reference to him wearing a nose ring.

The Arrival

Technology has advanced us beyond the paper road maps, and many traveled the distance to listen to the highly hyped 13th studio album of Shawn Carter. The scene at the Sprint Store for the TIDALXSprint Pop-Up Album release of 4:44 was standing room only with many standing outside enjoying the innovative introduction to 4:44 with the sounds of DJ QuickSilva on the 1's and 2's. Still not 100% certain as to what the whole 4:44 TIDAL means – that's called word play- but anyway, he will clear up any misconceptions or doubts.

The Doors Are Open

Luckily TIDAL is a music streaming source and not a GPS system because Downtown Silver Spring has been mapped out as DC now. Despite geographical locations, many people showed up ready for the release of 4:44, Shawn Carters 13th music studio album. Before Jay Z could arrive at the TIDALXSprint Pop Up he had to but in some major work, and now much has changed from his lifestyle to lyrics. Let's just reflect on America in the last 4 years and how his music has influenced the rap culture.

Four years after his 2013 "Magna Carter Holy Grail" studio release, Shawn Carter jumped on the campaign trail with HER. That didn't interfere with putting some "love on top" of his wife Beyonce' not once, but twice, and came out with three bundles of joy. Moving right along, then comes generating a buzz for "Black Lives Matter" where many marched across America holding up "Jobs, Justice, and Equality" signs instead of "It's the Rock" sign. After making a monetary contribution to the movement; which didn't resonate at the voting booth, Jay Z announced he would bail black men out of jail. Only for all of those efforts to result in a major sting – Donald Trump becomes President of the 2016 election.

Suppose Jay Z may have some subconscious challenges, but he managed to stay in position, and spark some life back into Al Sharpton's selfie game. The preacher should never have a bad photo that isn't worthy to be praised. In fact,, we should "Smile," beyond "Reasonable Doubt," since giving "The Blueprint," to now revealing on his 13th studio album his mother may be a lesbian. The delivery of that line is fitting and comes at a perfect time since the LGBT community is more acclimated in today's society prior to Al Sharpton's selfie days.

It's Time 4:44

The first track played at the TIDALXSprint Pop Up album release was "Kill Jay Z." Then

"4:44," "Smile," and, I stayed until "Bam!" After his 13th album, it's evident that Jay Z's marketing strategy has evolved. 4:44 was a more innovative approach, not sure if sales is the primary focus, but he has managed to leverage the new wave medium of online streaming. The source TIDAL has subscribers which offer exclusive services such as being able to stream the album from their smart phone, along with other offerings. This exclusive TIDALXSprint market merger's goal is to provide Sprint customers the opportunity to stream the online service for 6 months free of charge. This strategy secures the sales with the added value to shopping online. Most importantly this merger will support the 1 Million Project, an initiative that will connect 1 million low-income U.S. high school students who don't have internet access at home.

Adopting a Healthy Lifestyle, Nurturing the Mind, Body & Soul

Now that the weather has finally adjusted to a bearable temperature, taking a walk is not such a bad idea. Walking and working out are fun! In fact, it's phenomenal, simply because of the results.

DC Get Ready To "Leave It On the Floor"

With a mission and goal to honor Women, highlighting the importance of Women's Wellness and Fitness, PR WIZ, LLC presented the "Mind Body & Soul Women's Wellness Fitness Tour" featuring MixFitz Studio Mrs. Crystal Wall of Houston, Texas.

A perfect start to Mother's Day weekend, the MBSWWFT kicked off a Halftime Sports Bar, Saturday afternoon on H Street in Ward 5 DC. Although I exercise twice a week, watching Instagram fitness classes from your smart phone has a different affect in real life! Mrs. Wall introduced herself along with the #BAMFs. The first song I'm like "oh my" this is getting intense, but I can't stop now! Another attendee says "we are enjoying it, and we\'re about to die." Finally, a small break arrived for water, but not enough to cool you off; before it was time to *"leave it on the floor"* once more.

The Mind Body & Soul Women's Wellness Fitness Tour is important for many reasons beyond promoting the importance of Women's Wellness and Fitness. According to the National Center for Chronic Disease Prevention and Health Promotion Division, heart disease is the leading cause of death for African American and White Women in the United States. Other high risk factors include poor diet, and diabetes which is high levels of blood glucose resulting from defects in insulin production and action. The MBSWWFT is a perfect choice to aid in prevention of these leading causes of death among African American and White women in the US.

Through facilitating adopting a healthy lifestyle nurturing the mind, body, and soul; attendees enjoyed delicious delights delicately made by @thelifestyleshift who wanted to bless attendees with good greens goodness "Alive Salad". These greens were soaked in various plant-based foods versus ham hock.

A moment of motivation by author Beverly Smith-Brown, and engaged in over 60 minutes of high intense physical activity taught by Mrs. Crystal Wall. This tour was able to impact the District impart through collaborating with companies such as DTLR, Get Hemp Butter, and High Definition Society that understand the importance of Women's Wellness, adopting and maintaining a healthy lifestyle.

Supporting Women's Wellness

Although heart disease and diabetes are leading causes of death among Women in the United States, adopting a healthy lifestyle nurturing the mind body and soul are preventive measures.

Title: Tuesday Fashion Trends on time for spring

Interactive Source: Vimeo.com

Original Production Year: ***2017***

<u>MJ News Update</u>: I don't recall if Instagram is where we met, but instantly I knew Aaliyah would be perfect for the digital production. Without having a conversation about her fashion expertise, I knew she was the fashion forward person to bring the content to life. And it was true, she designs and has her own home décor line and more. Glad to use Instagram for outreach but the engagement was in real time and real life.

Fashion Trends in Time for spring with Fashionista Aaliyah B.

Even if your fashion sense Issa questionable, it's always a great time to talk fashion! Especially when the weather is right for those stunning spring and summer looks.

Help Issa on the Way

We can all admit, our style and taste for fashion is impeccable, and no one can't tell us that we don't look good! Personally, as long as it screams "*SALE*," in season or out of season I will make the purchase. Not sure if that\'s considered fashion forward or being a frugal shopper. Needless to say, we can all use some fashion pointers. Ladies, the perfect fashionista, Mrs. Aaliyah Brazile will help ease all stress by finding the stunning spring trends.

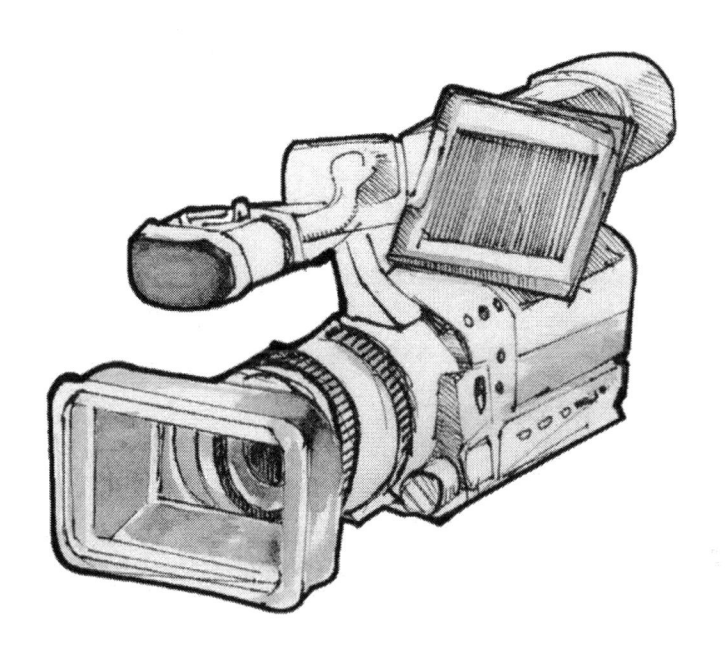

Title: Imagine Life without Art, it wouldn't be a beautiful sight

Interactive Source: Vimeo.com

Original Production Year: **2017**

MJ News Update: ART adds value and meaning to any space and without it we wouldn't know much about history. Most artist are sensitive about their creative works as they should be and advocating for the arts has always been a priority.

ART Matters

Could you imagine life without art? It would be quite awful. It's possibly safe to say no need to argue that thought. A world without art has no life.

Art is everything

There is no escaping art. From our home to our car, clothes, shoes, you name it! Some elements or art techniques were required. Furthermore, no Shakespeare, Romeo and Juliet, and forget about Hamilton. No need to purchase any Jean-Michel Basquiat.

Living in Washington, we are surrounded by art, from the architecture of the buildings like the monument to murals painted on alleyway walls, and ARTS ACTION DC wanted to remind the DC Council of the impact and importance of art so they should consider allocating more funding for arts programs and initiatives. Many arts advocates let their voice be heard at the Wilson Building meeting with Councilmembers. The main topics of the discussion were funding for DC Commission Arts and Humanities, financial support to implement the DC Cultural Plan along with developing new funding cohort for the Creative Economy.

Art is important because it tells the history of a culture and society. If no artifacts existed, then there would be no way to determine what role the pyramids in Egypt played in our society. For something so critical and a need in society, governing officials manage to cut funding for the arts first. Why is that? Perhaps they are always arguing about what legislation is more important. If we never needed art in America, the time is now. We must create a more beautiful world than building walls to keep people out.

Title: Who's Rights? Women & Transgender women

Interactive Source: Vimeo.com

Original Production Year: *2017*

MJ News Update: It's a lovely start to spring! What's most beautiful it's still Women's History Month! During this month Women are recognized for their many accomplishments, and contributions to communities in America and abroad. Should Transgender Women be given the same rights as Women? Why or why not? Tune in. Since this production, transgender women have received more protections and rights. The bathrooms have upgraded to gender neutral, so any gender is able to use them. Abortion rights have also been generating more buzz since the community has rights now.

Title: Whole Foods opens in Ward 5, who's going to giant?

Interactive Source: Vimeo.com

Original Production Year: ***2018***

MJ News Update: With inflation constantly rising, where you buy your groceries is important. Having a Whole Foods in the community is great, but the price points have increased drastically since 2018. The price of eggs in 2018 was under $5.00, and now the cost has doubled. Having a source for healthy food attributes to your lifestyle so be sure to learn about the grocer before giving them a payment.

Whole Foods Opens in Ward 5, Wonder Who's Going to GIANT?

Healthy eating in Ward 5

Whole Foods in now Open! What a healthy treat for the residents in Ward 5, Washington DC. Residents now have many alternatives for food shopping along the H Street corridor, starting with Giant grocery which is just about a block from Whole Foods, along with Safeway and ALDI.

Although Whole Foods is surrounded by much competition, what sets them aside from its competitors is that they don't allow hydrogenated fats or artificial colors, flavors, preservatives or sweeteners in any food they sell. Whole Foods standards give the best experience and products, and they consider quality the highest form of value. Well, you can most certainly spend some quality time in the lounge located upstairs, inside the Whole Foods on H Street, NE Ward 5.

Here's a tip! Get your coupons online before you go to the store!

Mindy's Monday Movie Review

Let's Get Right to It!

Many movies are at the theaters and chances are, most people's movie preference seems to be #GETOUT, considering box office sales of over $100 million. Don't forget the movie cost under $6 million to make, now that is what you call #nofraud. Furthermore, Jordan Peele's #GETOUT is a horror movie, with a Black male hero.

My friend took me to the Regal Cinema at Gallery Place in Chinatown DC. Luckily, he had already purchased the tickets. We walked up to the ticket attendant; he places his cellphone under the atom, and it read the ticket bar code. "Theater 13 to the left," was our destination, but before going to see #GETOUT, I had to get some nachos and cheese with jalapeno peppers and a large blue raspberry icee, in fact it was so large it had to be carried in a bag.

By the time we arrived at our seats in the very front row of the theater, literally, the opening movie credits were still rolling, and we were on time for #GETOUT. The character Chris Washington has many challenges to overcome. Starting with the startling death of his mother at a very young age. In the movie it is as though Chris had been searching for a lady to fill the void of his mother, and who better but a delicate Rose, respectful not mama Rosebud to tend to his needs and desires. As a photographer, Chris understands focus and the use of flash to capture a picture-perfect subject or image. Even though his last image was that of a wolf in the woods, jumping into the sky, he noticed it, but he really didn't pay it much attention because his focus was on Rose, and going to meet her family which already knew he was a Black man.

Along the way to meet Rose's parents, a deer hits them. That was significant in the sense; it's like one is running around like a deer with no sense of direction only for acceptance. Sometimes in life we are looking through two different lens, what we want our life to be, and what our reality is, and often times we can get hypnotized by people such as Rose only to end up in a place which we thought would be our security and comfort zone. Not only that, but everything could be taking away also, like your brain, if you are no paying attention and focused on the right things. Your brain can be taken and given to someone else to use against you.

Well, that is my review, be sure to go see the movie, and if you have, comment. I'd like to know what you think of the movie!